How to Die of Embarrassment Every Day

How to Die of Embarrassment Every Day

Ann Hodgman

Henry Holt and Company

New York

Henry Holt and Company, LLC
Publishers since 1866
175 Fifth Avenue
New York, New York 10010
mackids.com

Henry Holt® is a registered trademark of Henry Holt and Company, LLC.
Text copyright © 2011 by Ann Hodgman
All rights reserved.

Library of Congress Cataloging-in-Publication Data
Hodgman, Ann.
How to die of embarrassment every day / Ann Hodgman.—1st ed.
p.   cm.
ISBN 978-0-8050-8705-5
1. Hodgman, Ann—Childhood and youth—Juvenile literature.   2. Authors,
American—20th century—Biography—Juvenile literature.   3. Embarrassment
in children—Juvenile literature.   I. Title.
PS3558.O343446Z46 2011   818'.4309—dc22   [B]   2010049004

First Edition—2011
Book designed by Véronique Lefèvre Sweet
Printed in the United States of America by
R. R. Donnelley & Sons Company, Harrisonburg, Virginia

3 5 7 9 10 8 6 4 2

The author/editor and publisher gratefully acknowledge the permission granted to reproduce the
copyright material in this book.

Every effort has been made to trace copyright holders and to obtain their permission for the
use of copyright material. The publisher apologizes for any errors or omissions in the list below
and would be grateful if notified of any corrections that should be incorporated in future reprints
or editions of this book.

Image from Sears catalog, page 47,
reprinted by permission of Sears Holding Company.

Text and images from Brownie Handbook,
pages 150–58, reprinted by permission of Girl Scouts U.S.A.

Oh la la dee dee to Cootie, Lolo, and Nood

*   *   *

If I could go back and change one thing in my life,
I think it would be that time I found that one-dollar bill on
the sidewalk. I would change it to a million-dollar bill.
—Jack Handey, *Fuzzy Memories*

Table of Contents

How to Die of Embarrassment Every Day

The Rules Of This Book

This isn't a regular book. You don't have to read the chapters in order. As a matter of fact, they're not even exactly chapters. Some of them are so short that they're really more like paragraphs, or what magazine editors call "boxes." Some are so short that you would need a microscope to see them.

After all, it's not as if I had a really eventful childhood. I wasn't the type of kid people looked at and said, "She's going to be the first woman president." My life just went along, probably the way yours does. So what am I going to do for a book? Write things like "Then, next year, I was in third grade"? I don't want to give you my whole life story! I just want to give you some *little* life stories! I want to give you the, you know, *meat* of the sandwich, not the boring old bread. So if you want to find out dates and history and things, you'll have to wait until I die and then read my autobiography. Which I won't be writing, because it would be too boring. And also because I'll be dead.

Some of the names in this book are real, and some are fake. I bet you can guess which kind Miss Stinkyface is. (Real.) If I was describing something that might embarrass people I liked, or might make them feel bad, I didn't want to use real names. On the other hand, I figured it was okay to use real names when I wasn't talking about anything bad. On the *third* hand, I didn't want to use real names even for people I hated, because what if they turned nice later on? Or got mad and came after me?

Sometimes, just to keep things interesting, I used a person's real name in one part of the book and his or her fake name in another.

This book only goes up through sixth grade. After that, my life became so embarrassing that writing it down would have caused the pages to burst into flames. Like what about the time I wore a fake-leather pantsuit and big Pilgrim-looking shoes and a ruffled shirt to the mall in seventh grade, and people kept staring at me, and I finally called my mother to bring me some regular clothes to change into in the car? I still live in dread that someday, a person from my teenage past will threaten to tell my husband and kids alllllllllllllll about what I used to be like. If that happens, there won't be any point in my paying the blackmailer. I'll just have to change my name and move away.

Do You Like Me Yet?

Whatever's your first memory? Write it in the space below, and let's see if it's the same as mine.

Is it the time you were about two and a half and you lived in Germany with your parents because your dad was in the army?

And you reached up to the top of the stove to get your toy cow, which was up there drying because it had been washed, and you burned your wrist on the pilot light?

Here I am with that stupid toy cow. I guess this is how it got wet in the first place.

I thought so. I knew we had a lot in common.

And weren't you the kid who, like me, was reading in bed one summer night in your calm suburban neighborhood and leaning up against the windowsill to catch the last remaining light when a bullet *zizzed* through the windowpane right next to your face? And you ran downstairs and told the babysitter (because your parents were out to dinner), "I think a bullet just came through my window"? And she said, "How do you know?"? And you said, "I was reading in bed, and it came right past me"? And the sitter said, "That goes to show that you shouldn't read in bed"?

Wait. Maybe that only happened to me. We found the bullet under my bed the next morning. It turned out that a bad kid down the block had shot a gun into a swimming pool, and the bullet had ricocheted up all that way to come through my window. The kid's punishment was supposed to be helping put in a new pane of glass, but he never did it. And I never stopped reading in bed, either.

But of course my childhood wasn't ALL burns and bullets. Most of it was nice and ordinary, just like yours. Just like you, I was supposed to walk the dog in the mornings before school. And, *exactly* like you, I had a special song I liked to sing during these walks, one I had composed for the occasion. It had what I liked to imagine was a haunting melody, and it went like this:

Walk on this side, pup,
Not on that side, pup,
Oh, you have a lot of things to learn.
Learn to heel, pup,
Learn to sit down, pup,
Oh, you have a lot of things to learn.

I sang nice and loudly, which must have been a treat for our neighbors early in the morning. And why was I so loud? Because I suspected that a movie director might be driving through our neighborhood just around that time. Where *else* would a movie director want to be at seven in the morning but Rochester, New

York? And when he heard me singing—and singing a song I had composed myself!—I was pretty sure he'd put me into one of his movies.

Back in my childhood, biographies were one of the main things we checked out of the school library. The biographies I liked best were published by a company called Bobbs-Merrill, and they were all about famous people when they were kids. Of course, there were a lot of famous people who hadn't done much as kids, so the writers had to make stuff up. They could get away with it, because how was anyone going to check their facts? For a biography of, say, George Washington, a Bobbs-Merrill biography might have a bunch of chapters about how honest and independent George had been as a boy. The cherry tree he had supposedly chopped down would be in there, but maybe also some stuff about George being chosen leader of his playmates. "You should be in charge, George," his friends in the book might say. "You seem born to command." Then the last chapter in the book would be something like, "Later, George grew up to be the first president of the United States. The End." (I'm exaggerating a little, but not much.)

Anyway. In second grade I read a Bobbs-Merrill biography of Juliette Low, the founder of the Girl Scouts. In it I learned that during the Civil War, the Low family—who were from Savannah—were "rebels" who believed in the Southern cause. This astonished me. I couldn't believe that someone whose biography I was reading could actually be on the wrong side in the Civil War. Imagine! The founder of the Girl Scouts, an actual *rebel*! For days after I read the book, I walked around muttering, "The Rebels and the Yankees. The Rebels and the Yankees." I was hoping that some grown-up would ask, "What did you say, Ann?" And then I would be

Juliette **Low**
GIRL SCOUT

by Helen Boyd Higgins

"That's why people think we're Yankees. I wish you had told him to stay away. I wish I hadn't eaten that old sugar he brought for Nellie and me. Just the same, it was good and I never saw sugar before."

"Now, Daisy, let me talk, dear," said Mrs. Gordon. "When General Sherman was here I asked permission to go through his lines to visit our Southern soldiers. I wanted to see Papa.

The general said I might and gave me a pass. I saw Papa last night."

"You went right through the Yankee army? Wasn't that exciting, Mamma? You saw Papa and we didn't! That wasn't fair," cried Daisy. "Is he coming home right away? Tell me quick."

"I will, Juliette, if you'll just be quiet," said Mrs. Gordon.

Daisy put her hand over her mouth and nodded. When Mamma called her by her real name she knew she must mind.

"Papa wants you and Nellie and baby Alice and me to go on a long visit to Chicago, to see Grandpa and Grandma Kinzie. We'll go on a boat which will take us to New York. General Sherman said it would be all right. We'll take a train from New York to Chicago. We are going today!"

Daisy couldn't speak for a second. She had so many questions she didn't know which to ask

15

able to explain that in the Civil War there were two sides—the Rebels and the Yankees—and that Juliette Low had been a little rebel. How smart I would look, knowing all about the Civil War like that!

You did that too, right? And you wished you could have been Helen Keller because she was always the center of attention?

Oh. You didn't?

But you always wanted to know a girl who did stuff like that, right? And who really, really cared what kind of toothpaste her friends used—Crest or Colgate—and always made a point of asking new friends "What kind of toothpaste do you use?" And you would have wanted a girl like that for your best friend, right?

. . . Oh. I see. Hmmm.

Well, I hope you'll still give me a try.

Where It All Started

When I used to read aloud to my children, Laura and John, I sometimes had to warn them that the first part of a book might be boring. It's a lot of work setting up a story. You have to bring in most of the major characters and describe where the book is set and talk about anything else the readers have to know before you start the action. So it's fine with me if you go ahead and skip the next few pages; I give you absolute permission.

Because I'm sure you don't care about background things like where I grew up, and why should you? But it was in Rochester, New York. My dad was studying to be a doctor at the University of Rochester, and he and my mother and my little sister Cathy and I lived near the hospital. The apartment complex where we lived until I was six was called University Park. All the dads were studying at the University of Rochester; all the mothers were moms. If there were any graduate-student mothers, we never knew them. Most of the moms were either pregnant or had a baby in addition to what I thought of as their "real" children.

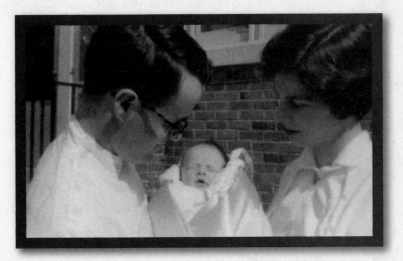

The cutest baby in the world, with her adoring parents.
I wonder if you can guess her name.

My best friends at University Park were Benjy Sax, who was my age, and his younger sister, Anne, who was a year older than my sister Cathy. (There were a lot of Annes and Anns back then, just as there are a lot of Emmas and Hannahs now. There were also a lot of Barbaras, Susans, Marys, and Debbies.) Mrs. Sax smoked cigarettes, which made me jealous. I wished my mother smoked too, so that I could have played with the smoke that swirled and coiled into the air so fascinatingly. Also, Benjy and Anne got to call their mother Mommy or Mom, whereas I had to say Mummy or Mum. My mother claimed that Mum was what kids said in Boston, where she had grown up. Of course by the time I noticed that I was different from other kids on this matter, Mum had come to seem like my mother's real name—but saying it in front of other kids made me feel like a foreigner.

Also, the Saxes had a TV, and we didn't.

We lived in a first-floor two-bedroom apartment. When I was three, I liked to scrub the path outside the apartment with leaves. The leaves turned the concrete a faint green, and the scrubbing turned the leaves into shredded nets of tissue. "Look, Mum and Dad," I would say, holding up a leaf. "A holey leaf! Get it?" I had the idea that "holy" and "full of holes" meant the same thing and that I was making a pun. At the same age, my future husband, David Owen, got confused and thought the word "eggnog" meant "garbage." "Quit throwing that eggnog into my yard!" he told the girls next door.

The Saxes lived in a second-floor apartment around the corner from us. Once, in the night, I woke up and found that my parents weren't home. That's not a thing you like to discover when you're little. Leaving Cathy sleeping, I went out in my nightgown and ran to the Saxes' apartment for help. There, turning their startled faces toward me, were my parents, who had just gotten some bad news about a friend. That same year, my mother's mother died. I can remember watching my mother cry and feeling vaguely irritated and scared at the same time. *Mothers* weren't supposed to walk around crying. To cheer Mum up, I let out a big fake sob and said, "See? I can cry too!"

A few apartments down from mine, the sidewalk became rough and broken for half a block. My friends and I called that part the Bumpity Sidewalk. I had a big old secondhand tricycle with a front wheel that was big enough for me to sit on while Benjy Sax pedaled me around. One morning, while Benjy was pedaling and I was riding, Benjy said, "We're coming to the Bumpity Sidewalk. Better lift up your feet." I stuck my right foot into the spokes of my tricycle to move it out of the way and got a big cut on my foot that had to be stitched up at what we always called Dad's Hospital. When a nurse rinsed the cut, the water in the basin turned a cloudy pink.

Down the street from University Park was a little house where another medical-school family, the Thalers, lived. David Thaler was my age—well, three days younger than I. (He lives on a kibbutz in Israel now, but we e-mail each other on our birthdays every year.) Our favorite game was pretending to be Babar and Celeste, from the Babar books: David was Babar, of course, and I was Celeste. My sister Cathy, who was about a year and a half old, was Arthur. Cathy got confused about this sometimes. She would walk around saying, "I not Arthur. I Cathy. I not Cathy. I Arthur."

At other times Cathy could be very clearheaded. Once David, his older brother and sister, and Cathy and I were all playing in his backyard while our mothers had coffee in the kitchen. At some point, Cathy must have gotten bored. When my mother checked on us through the Thalers' kitchen window, Cathy was nowhere in sight. I hadn't noticed her leaving the yard, but I still remember the tremendous flurry created by her disappearance— and no wonder. My mother left me with the Thalers while she rushed off to look for Cathy. This was before we had a car, so she had to search on foot. Knowing Cathy's ways, Mum decided to check our apartment first. There she found Cathy playing all by herself. She had headed down the Thalers' block, crossed a busy street alone, walked to our apartment, and brought in the mail as she went inside. Later, Cathy's nursery school teacher said, "Cathy is the most logical four-year-old I've ever seen."

My other hero besides Babar was Mighty Mouse, who was on TV on Saturday mornings. We watched him at the Saxes' apartment. How I loved Mighty Mouse! I had an actual crush on him, and once, when I was nine, I had an actual *dream* that he rescued me and flew me through the air in his strong mouse arms. This was years after I had stopped watching the show, but I guess Mighty Mouse was still lodged in my brain somewhere. When the show was over—it was on from ten to ten thirty—all the little boys in University Park would come rushing outside with towels tied around their shoulders to make capes. (Not the girls. It would never have occurred to us.) For the next hour or so, until lunchtime, dozens of Mighty Mice jumped and swooped around the playground.

No one locked doors during the daytime then, and—as I guess may already be sort of obvious—kids weren't supervised as strenuously as they are now. As soon as you turned five or so in University Park, you could just go out and play wherever you wanted. That's why my mom wasn't there to stop me when I decided to push over Dwight Jacobs's snowman one winter morning. I can still remember walking by his apartment in my snowsuit and thinking, "We've seen that snowman for long enough." Dwight's mother rushed out to yell at me, and later I had to go back and apologize to Dwight.

I broke another law at the Pic'n'Pay, the little grocery store down the street from University Park. The mothers often took us there, and one day Mrs. Sax brought me and *her* Anne along while she got some milk. "Can we have some candy?" I asked her. There were bins of penny candy near the cash register. Mrs. Sax said no and walked down the aisle to the milk cooler in back. I said to Anne, "Let's just take some." (Anne was four, and I was five, so I felt free to boss her around.) We reached into the bins, grabbed a handful of Red Hot Dollars, and stuffed them into our mouths. Mrs. Sax was not pleased, and neither was the store owner. That was another time I had to go back and apologize. Is there anything as scary as that?

My mother, Joanna Bailey, when she was about your age or a little younger. *She* never stole anything from *Pic'n'Pay.*

Wait! Yes, there is! It's equally scary when you're at a friend's house—let's say her name is Laurie—and her mother suddenly calls, "Laurie, could you come in here, please?" Both of you can tell from the mom's voice that Laurie's in trouble of some kind.

"Come with me! Come with me!" begs Laurie in a whisper. She's thinking that with you there, her mother won't be able to yell as hard. So, out of loyalty, you go with her, and it turns out she was wrong: her mother is able to yell *just* as hard.

Let's See, What Else Happened at University Park?

I knew a brother and sister named Richard and Gretchen. I called them both Ritchen and named my doll Ritchen after them. She was a big, realistic baby doll about the same size as a six-month-old, so she could wear real baby clothes. She was made of molded plastic, and I didn't love her quite as much after some of her toes chipped off and I could see into her hollow foot.

A neighbor down the street found a kitten under her sofa, and we all trooped in to look at it. I've never wanted anything in my life as much as that kitten.

When I was three, my mother asked me to put some towels in the bathroom for her. I said, "Work, work, work! When will I ever get my rest?"

In my first year of preschool, I learned a Thanksgiving song that went:

♪ *A turkey ran away upon Thanksgiving Day,*
"I fear," said he, "I'd roasted be if I should stay." ♪

I came home from school, and in a high, shrill voice (I always believed that the higher a voice was, the prettier it sounded), I sang with great assurance

> ♪ *A turkey ran away before Thanksgiving Day.* ♫
> *I hee he said, I roasted be if I should stay."*

Puzzled, my parents asked me to sing the second line again.

"I hee he said, I roasted be if I should stay,'" I repeated.

"Ann, that can't be right," said Dad. "It doesn't make any sense."

"*Yes!* That's the way it *goes!*" I insisted. "My teacher said so!" It was the first time I had ever used my teacher as an authority against my parents.

At the same age, my son, John, sang the *Teenage Mutant Ninja Turtles* cartoon theme song this way:

> ♫ *T-U Minga Minga Turtles,*
> *Heroes in the half-shell! Turtle power!* ♪
> *When the evil Shredder attacks,*
> ♫ *These turtle boys don't cunnem no syce!*

That last line was supposed to be "These turtle boys don't cut him no slack!" There was also a line about Raphael being "cool but crude" that John sang as "Raphael is cool but poo" and a line about Michaelangelo's being a "party dude" that John sang as "Michaelangelo to the party time!" But let's get back to me.

I was extremely afraid of robbers. If I happened to hear a car outside at night, I was always sure it was some robbers preparing to sneak into our apartment. I would lie awake in bed, tense with fear, and promise myself, "When I'm ten years old, I won't be afraid of robbers anymore." Unfortunately, at ten I *was* still afraid of them, so I had to up the age to fifteen. That time it worked.

I was also afraid of kidnappers, of course. We all were, except for Lisa Olsen down the street. When Lisa was four, her mother gave her the usual speech about how if someone tries to make you go into his car, you *must come home right away.* Later that morning, Lisa came in and said cheerfully, "No one tried to make me get into their car, but I just came home anyway."

I was also afraid of the illustrations in a library book about a hippopotamus who got sad for some reason. The pictures had too much purple and black and too many swirly lines. One night I woke up crying, "I just hate those pictures!"

Benjy Sax and I both got a nickel for allowance, because we were five years old. Anne Sax was only four, so her allowance was four cents. Cathy was still too little to have an allowance.

My first Halloween costume was a brown paper shopping bag that I wore over my head, with eyes cut into it.

The main thing that happened in University Park was that my sister Cornelia—called Nelie—was born. My sister Cathy had always been there as far as I knew, but I definitely remember Nelie's birth. Dad had to take care of me and Cathy while Mum was in the hospital. At breakfast he burned the scrambled eggs—not a lot, but scrambled eggs don't have to be very burned for you to notice. At night Dad made us hamburgers, and they caught on fire. The next day, he took us on a picnic in a field somewhere, and we picked wild strawberries that Dad took to my mother when he visited her in the hospital. (Children weren't allowed to visit maternity wards back then.) And that night, when Cathy and I were lying in our beds talking, Cathy said, "When the new baby comes home, I'm not going to let you hold her."

Me, holding Cornelia, and Cathy looking wistfully on wishing *she* were still the baby.

"You have to!" I said, shocked. "We *both* get to hold her. Mum said."

"Not you. I'm not letting you."

I can't believe I started crying. I was five and a half, and Cathy was only three!

My poor father came storming in. "What's going on in here?" he asked. When I blubbered out Cathy's cruelty, Dad also couldn't believe I was so upset. "If she told you the moon was made of green cheese, would you believe her?" he said crossly.

"No, but—"

"I want both of you to go to sleep right now," said my father.

Speaking of babies reminds me of one more thing about University Park. I once came home for lunch and announced, "I asked Mrs. DiPietro where babies come from, but she said she doesn't know."

The First Move

At the end of second grade, my parents told me we were moving to a Rochester suburb called Brighton. Of course I didn't want to move there. I didn't even like to go into a room if my parents had changed the furniture around.

"I don't like how Brighton sounds," I said.

"It's a very nice town," my mother reassured me.

"A TOWN?" I shrieked. "I don't want to live in a TOWN!"

The only town I knew was the picture on my box of tiny German building blocks. Suddenly I was sure that my parents were moving us somewhere foreign-seeming with red wooden roofs. Maybe there were even canals there, like in Holland! But it turned out that we moved to a regular street called Cobb Terrace, with regular houses and kids on it. Our house had a huge pine tree in front, with a big, low branch that three or four kids could bounce around on. We named the branch Merbeth, after a childhood cousin of my father's.

Nelie had her own bedroom next to my parents' room. Cathy and I shared a bedroom with complicated yellow-and-white wallpaper. When we took our naps, we were never sleepy, and we would lie on our beds kicking and staring at the walls. Once, to vary the boringness, I suggested that we trade beds at naptime. The next afternoon, Cathy said, "I don't want to nap on your bed anymore. You don't have any faces in your wallpaper."

I was confounded for two reasons. First, the wallpaper was exactly the same next to both beds. Second, while I'd been lying on Cathy's bed, I had felt as though I couldn't find any faces in *her* wallpaper. How could both things be true?

It was on Cobb Terrace that Nelie spent a whole summer wearing a bathing cap because she liked the look of bathing caps,

My sister Nelie loved bathing caps.

and Cathy and I went outside one hot day wearing just bloomers and no shirts. Bloomers, in case you didn't know, are like fancy, puffed underpants that you wear over your *real* underpants. No one in real America still wore them except us—they were only seen in Boston. (That stupid Boston! It got us into so much trouble!) Cathy and I had gone out in just bloomers at University Park, but we soon realized that on Cobb Terrace, wearing only bloomers was practically as bad as going outside naked. The mean boy next door, Jimmy Manson, said, "Do you like bacon?"

"Yes," I said, puzzled.

"Wanna strip?"

That was a bad moment.

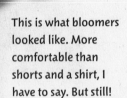

This is what bloomers looked like. More comfortable than shorts and a shirt, I have to say. But still!

It was on Cobb Terrace that we got our first dog, Slats. "He's going to the toilet," said my grandma Donna once when we were walking Slats.

"No, he's not," Cathy corrected her. "He's going to the grass."

Cobb Terrace was where I did my first cooking, making witches' brew. I stood on a chair at the stove and filled a big pot with water and all the spices I could find, plus bouillon cubes and a little molasses and some vinegar and salt and baking powder. The whole spices and bay leaves bobbed at the surface of the water, and the bouillon cubes and molasses made it brown, and a little bit of froth formed on the top when the brew began to boil, and it was very witchy and satisfying. Then I dared my father to try some, and he did! And he said he liked it!

It was on Cobb Terrace that mean Jimmy Manson hit Slats with a snow shovel, and on Cobb Terrace that Slats died a few months later. (From distemper, not from being hit with the shovel. Also, in fairness I should mention that Jimmy Manson got nice later.) It was there that my brother, Ned, was born when I was seven. When Ned was still teeny—less than a month old—we moved to our real house, 64 Monteroy Road, and my real life began.

My Animals—Live, Dead, and Stuffed

Here I am with one of our dogs, Gay. I'm the one who is vacantly staring out.

In second grade, I went shopping with my friend Kim Nichols and her mom. Kim was a friend whose younger sister had needed to get a tetanus shot after accidentally sitting down on a rake. That same younger sister had once told my younger sister Cathy, "*N-O* spells no" when Cathy was playing over there and said she wanted to go home. Anyway, while Kim and her mother and I were walking toward the department store, a woman passed us with a dog on a leash.

"What a strange-looking dog," said Mrs. Nichols.

"It's a Dandie Dinmont, I believe," I said suavely.

"Ann, you're full of surprises," said Mrs. Nichols. At the time, I thought it was a compliment.

As far as I was concerned, why *not* read a guide to dog breeds? It was just as interesting as any other book, and it would help me show off. Even though I was wrong about Dandie Dinmonts— the dog we saw was a Sealyham, I later realized. But I never told Mrs. Nichols I had made a mistake.

When I wasn't thinking about my other usual interests as a kid, I was thinking about animals. I think this started when I was a baby; I have a postcard from my father telling me how much I would have loved seeing some wasps he had noticed somewhere in Texas. ("From a distance," Dad added.) I was about eighteen months old when he sent me the card. I don't think he would have thought to mention something like wasps if he hadn't already noticed how much I liked animals.

And by animals I also mean parts of animals. It's hard for me to believe now how much I loved my rabbit's foot when I was in preschool. I don't mean the foot of my living pet rabbit. I mean a keychain made from a dead rabbit's foot, with little toenails and everything. If I saw one of those now, I'd feel sort of sick and sort of sad. But not back then! Back then, I really believed that if I couldn't have a real rabbit, a real rabbit's *foot* was the next best thing. I carried that keychain around with me everywhere and patted it as if it was alive.

Same with my toy cat, Catty, whose fur made her seem extra real to me. Teddy, Dalmationy, and Catty were the three stuffed animals I kept in my bed. I don't know how kids end up choosing the toys they sleep with—or, in the case of my daughter and son, the blankets they slept with. Laura had a white crocheted blanket named Nanny and a green crocheted blanket named Green Nanny; John had a bunch of flannel baby blankets that he collectively called his Diddies. The Diddies have disappeared over the years, but Laura still has both her Nannies, as well as her old stuffed unicorn named Pony. Green Nanny lives with her, and regular Nanny is on her old bed in our house.

In my case, Teddy had always been there. He was a Steiff bear my parents got for me when we lived in Germany. He was actually a replacement; my original teddy bear had been stolen when my mother took me into a store and we left Teddy outside in my stroller. Nowadays a Steiff bear that size costs hundreds of dollars, but in Germany, in the 1950s, Teddy was a normal price. He had a little blue suit with a belt made of blue string. Once, on a long car trip, I tied the belt into many tiny knots to make it fancier. Teddy was much better than Dalmationy, whose fur soon wore off until he looked like a spotted washcloth, and who had the kind of plastic googly eyes that got scratched easily. (Dalmationy, I believed, was weak and sickly and needed special attention.) But Catty was covered with real fur, which made her almost as good as a real cat.

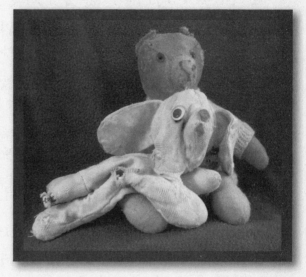

Of course, I still have Teddy and Dalmationy. Teddy is wearing a handsome sweater to cover his no-fur-ness. Dalmationy looks even worse than he used to: mice have pulled out some of his stuffing over the years.

"Is this cat fur?" I asked hopefully when I got Catty for my fourth birthday.

"Rabbit, I think," said Mum.

Oh, well. Rabbit was almost as good, and at least the fur was real. It looked nice for a long time, too; it didn't get clumped and dirty like Dalmationy's fake plushy fur. It looked nice right up until I spat some shellac-tasting cough syrup all over it. We sponged Catty off, but she always had a reddish stain on the skin under her fur. (Because it was real fur, it was attached to real skin.) Then Catty's fur started to wear away. I didn't like the look of the bald, leathery patches of skin, so I put her into a cloth bag and sewed the top of it around her neck. I thought it would make her look as if she was peeking out of a sleeping bag, but it just looked creepy. Gradually, I started shoving her out of the way when I went to bed at night. In the morning, I would find her on the floor. And then one day—as my husband would put it—she became lost.

Again, I wasn't adding things up the way I would now. Now, with my adult, trained brain, I would look at a toy like Catty and think, "How horrible to use animal fur for a toy." But then? Never occurred to me. Let's hope it was just because I had a good imagination.

Although if you really love animals (and I love them so much that I once wrote a whole book about my pets), seeing them dead *is* still interesting. It's better than not seeing them at all, anyway. A few years ago, I was driving along with my kids when I realized that there was a dead porcupine on the side of the road. It must have been hit by a car. Well, none of us had ever seen a porcupine—up close or far away, living or dead—so I stopped the car, and we got out to get a better look. I suppose we wouldn't have looked too closely if the poor thing's body had been bashed up by the car, but it was still "whole." We even pulled out a few of its quills to take home. I made the kids wash their hands when we got home, of course. I may be the kind of person who would pull out a dead porcupine's quills, but I'm not completely senseless.

I had to be explained out of a few of my animal ideas when I was little. "Dad," I asked my father when I was seven, "if I hit a squirrel with a rock, can I nurse it back to health?"

"Of course not!" I was surprised at how shocked my father sounded. "That wouldn't be right at all. You can't hurt an animal just so you can help it."

My ears could hear his words, and my brain could understand them, but nothing about them made sense to me. I wanted so, so badly to be able to help a hurt wild animal that I would have done anything to get one under my control.

Besides, What About Insects?

One reason I was confused about the squirrel-and-rock discussion was that only a year earlier, my dad had helped me collect butterflies. How different was that from hitting a squirrel with a rock, I wondered? My friend Eric Olson and I were obsessed with collecting butterflies and moths when we were in first grade. And collecting butterflies means . . . I hate to say it . . . killing them. At least that's how we did it.

I would catch a butterfly in my butterfly net, and my father would carefully put it into a jar that held a cotton ball soaked in ether. In a minute or so, the butterfly would stop flapping and die, and then we would pin it to a piece of cardboard. I would carefully label the cardboard with the butterfly's name and then forget all about it. I have no idea what happened to those little pieces of cardboard. Maybe they're in a famous science museum somewhere!

I think that Eric actually grew up to be some kind of scientist. Luckily for the butterfly population, I lost interest in killing butterflies after a few months. Instead, I started a butterfly hospital. I became inspired in this direction when I noticed that many of the butterflies I caught in my net seemed to have been hurt during the catching process. And why not, with a seven-year-old girl bashing a net down on top of them? Their wings would get damaged, or they'd lose a foot. To help them, I would make a tiny batch of sugar water. Gripping the butterflies firmly by their wings, I would hold an eyedropper filled with sugar water up to their mouths. Their long, rolled-up tongues would unspiral to drink the liquid; then they'd roll back up again. Then I would put the injured butterflies into a jar "to recover."

Only I don't remember that any of them recovered. And again, why would they, with a seven-year-old pinching them by the wings and feeding them a liquid that had much, much more sugar than anything they could have found in nature? I'm going to stop thinking about this now.

On summer evenings, our lawn was filled with dozens of white moths about half an inch long. These were about as interesting as bits of flying Kleenex. Still, you could get a minute or two of fun from catching them in your cupped hands and looking at them up close before letting them go. No point in doing anything with them, though—they were too boring. Somehow I never liked moths as much as butterflies, anyway. I thought it seemed defective that they couldn't hold their wings up straight, the way butterflies can.

I was very interested in several kinds of moth caterpillars, though—especially woolly bears, which are the caterpillar of the tiger moth. Woolly bears are the *best* kind of caterpillar. They have a thick coating of bristly fur—black at each end, with a band of chestnut (the *best* color of brown) in the middle. People always say that the width of the chestnut band shows how hard the winter will be, but that's not true. It just tells you how late the caterpillar hatched earlier that year. Not that I know *how* it tells you that.

Where I live now, I see woolly bears all the time in the fall—scurrying across the road or bustling to get out of the way of my raking the lawn. But when I was little, I usually saw only one or two per fall. I loved picking them up; they'd roll into a compact little circle at first, then gradually unroll and begin investigating my hand. Woolly bear caterpillars "overwinter"—that is, they build their cocoons in the fall and hatch out in the spring. One year, Dad helped me set up a windowpane enclosure for a woolly bear caterpillar we found. We filled a cardboard box with leaves, tucked the caterpillar inside, and taped the box to the window in my bedroom, where we hoped it would be cold enough for the caterpillar to develop through the winter. I don't remember what happened, which means that probably nothing happened. I bet I got impatient and took the box down too early.

From Butterflies to Birds

In third grade, I got interested in writing poetry about birds. I don't know what put the idea into my head, but it definitely wasn't a class activity. Nevertheless, it was something I worked on at school. I would never have worked so hard on a project at home, where there was no one to give me a grade for it.

Secretly, I didn't think of the bird poems as mere poems. I thought of them as my "bird sequence." *The Bird Sequence of Ann Hodgman, Room 11.* There are so many to choose from that I don't know where to start. Actually, there are only six, but I still don't know where to start. Each is more magnificent than the next. Like "Oriole Among the Buttercups":

Little fairy emperor,
Little fairy king,
Skims among the yellow-gold
Ready for 'most anything!
Skims along the yellow-gold,
Without een a glance at one pink,
You are a very cunning bird,
I think!

Will your freindship
Come to an end?
Little bird, do not leave me.
You are my best freind!

There are a few problems here, besides the fact that I spelled "friend" wrong.

First of all, orioles don't fly "among the buttercups." They live in trees. Their nests, which they weave into little bags that hang from tree branches, are what they're famous for. So why did I go on about the buttercups that way?

And what's that thing about "without e'en a glance at *one* pink"? Pinks are a garden flower. (Guess what color they usually are?) If an oriole were flying among buttercups, which he wouldn't be, he wouldn't be anywhere near any pinks. Also, who says "e'en" nowadays, or e'en back in the days when I was a kid?

And also, I did not have an oriole as a best friend, or even a best friend. I had never seen an oriole in my life. I had only read about them in bird books. On the other hand, I had seen blue jays a ton of times, but you'd never know it from reading "The Bluejay":

O bluejay!
As your sky-blue coat shimmers,
Your crest shakes ever so slightly;
Are you preparing to fly off?

Your bright eye glances round,
Ready to do mischeif;
The white tip of your tail cocks a little,
Was there ever more a pretty bird!
Night comes near,
And you gather up,
And slip into the stars.

I'm not trying to be mean to myself. I realize that in some ways, these poems are pretty good for an eight-year-old, even if an eye can't "do mischeif." But in most ways, they're EXTREMELY TERRIBLE FOR ANYONE OF ANY AGE, because they're not real. I wasn't even using my imagination when I wrote them. I wasn't imagining what it would be like to be a bird, or coming up with real ways to describe birds, or even thinking about what I was saying. Mostly, I was just loving the idea of myself as a Great Bird Poet. It makes me want to go back into the past and slap myself.

The Chick

A few years ago, I overheard a little girl telling her father, "Daddy, Susie said she doesn't like our chick." That cracked me up, for some reason.

Anyway, I could have gotten a whole library's worth of poems—sad poems—about the chick I hatched the following year, in fourth grade. I had always wanted to hatch chicks in an incubator, and in fourth grade I somehow managed to persuade my wonderful teacher, Miss Swang, that it would be a good classroom project for us if I brought in an incubator and we hatched some eggs. A boy in the class knew where to get fertilized chicken eggs and said he'd bring some in if I provided the incubator. So then all I had to do was somehow persuade my father to help me build one—I mean, to build it all by himself while I watched and asked excited questions about whether we would be able to keep any of the chicks and how long it would take for them to hatch and how, yes, I knew that our house wouldn't really be the right place for chickens to live, but couldn't we just keep one hen and one rooster, or just one *hen*? Couldn't she have a nest in the garage?

Despite my pestering, Dad did get the incubator done at last.

I don't know where he found the plans for it, but it was very impressive. It was made of a cardboard box lined with fiberglas insulation, and there was a lightbulb in one corner to keep the incubator temperature at 99 degrees. Dad drove me to school with it, and we put the eggs inside and waited.

No one in my fourth-grade class knew anything about eggs, including Miss Swang. And why should she have? She was a teacher, not a poultry farmer. We also didn't know that every evening, after school had let out, the school janitor unplugged the incubator and then plugged it in again the next morning just before school started. He thought it was a fire hazard, which it may well have been. All the same, on the twenty-second day of the eggs' incubation, we suddenly heard faint cheeping and tapping sounds coming from one of them. A real chick was inside, ready to come out, almost right on schedule!

When we left school that afternoon, we were all sure that a fluffy yellow chick would be running around the incubator the next morning. But the next morning, the eggs were all still whole and the cheeping was still going on. I don't know whether it was Miss Swang or I who decided that the chick was too weak to get out of the shell by itself—I have a horrible feeling that I was the one—but whoever it was was wrong. It takes awhile for baby birds to emerge from their shells, and the cheeping and pecking are part of the process. The chicks aren't calling for help, as I imagined when I was little; they're just waking up and signaling to the mother hen that they're alive in there. You're absolutely supposed to leave the eggs alone for the last few days of their incubation.

But since none of us knew that, we called our school principal, Mr. Root—I guess because a principal is supposed to be able to help with *anything*. Mr. Root said he had grown up on a farm, which now I'm not so sure about, because if he had, wouldn't he have told us to leave the eggs alone? (Root really was his last name, though. I'm not making it up, even though it does sound awfully farmery.) Instead, as we all gathered around, Mr. Root picked up the egg and carefully flaked away the shell.

The chick inside was wet, sticky-looking, and grayish, but it was alive—the only one of the eggs to have produced a chicken. We knew that chicks start out kind of icky, so we weren't worried. We all kept running to check on him as he lay on his side. He didn't seem to be perking up much, but when we went outside for recess we were sure, once again, that when we came back inside he would be fluffy, yellow, and busy.

Except that when we came back inside, the chick was lying motionless with his head in his water dish. *That* didn't seem right. Miss Swang put out a finger and gingerly flicked the chick's head out of the dish, but he didn't move.

That was the end of our chick experiment. I felt squeamish

about my part in it for years. I hadn't exactly done anything wrong, but somehow I felt that my eagerness and impatience were what had killed the chick. If I hadn't wanted an incubator so badly, none of this would have happened.

The funny thing is that I still want an incubator. I have a lot of pet finches now, and I like to watch them sit on their eggs and hatch out babies—but one of these days I'm going to buy a little incubator and hatch a button quail.

In the meantime, I can always visit the baby ducks at my kids' old school, where the kindergarten teachers use an incubator to hatch a batch of ducklings every year. A few years ago, I went to visit the kindergarten class and see the new ducklings. They were scrambling all around their box, jumping in and out of their water—no drowning this time!—and being 100 percent fluffy and adorable.

A kindergarten girl pointed at something in the ducks' water. "What's *that*?" she asked me in a loud, excited voice.

"Well, honey, I'm afraid that ducks sometimes poop in their water," I said.

"They do," said the kindergarten teacher tiredly. "We've already talked about it."

Incubators are stressful for teachers, I guess. But as soon as I mentioned button quail a couple of paragraphs ago, I went on the computer and ordered an incubator from an online farm-equipment store. When it gets here, I'm going to order some button quail eggs. This time, I promise to leave the eggs alone until they've all hatched. And this time it's going to work, because now that I'm a grown-up, I know *everything*.

Here's me, pretending I know everything, in the Christmas card picture my parents sent out when I was in the third grade.

Things I Wanted

If you've ever read the Henry Huggins books by Beverly Cleary, you may have noticed how much more stuff you have than Henry. One whole book, *Henry and Beezus*, revolves around Henry's campaign to get a bike. A bike! To many American kids nowadays, a bicycle is a given. I'm not lecturing you about how privileged you are. I'm just saying that a bike is something lots of kids usually have automatically, like socks. Maybe you have to wait until Christmas or your birthday to get one, but you get one. And when you outgrow it, you usually get another one. It may not be the fanciest model, but you do have a bike.

Compare that with Henry Huggins's troubles in *Henry and*

Beezus. Practically every chapter is about his latest scheme to get a bicycle. At one point, Henry even thinks about putting a broomstick on a girl's bike so it will look like a boy's. When you read the book nowadays, you almost want to say, "Yeah, but why don't your parents just *buy you a bike*?" But that wasn't the way things worked back then.

And another thing: there's no snack food in the Henry Huggins books. Henry is always making himself a sandwich when he gets home from school, and once Beezus has a *cabbage core* as a snack. A cabbage core! My *tortoises* won't even eat cabbage! And the book says Beezus is too polite to gnaw on the cabbage in front of Henry. Why? Would he have wanted some?

The first Henry Huggins book was published in 1950, and I was born in 1956. (Yes, I realize that 1956 sounds like a fake year to you, but being born in the 1990s and the 2000s sounds fake to me.) My parents had more money than Henry's parents did. At least, I always thought Henry and his friend Beezus sounded sort of poor when I read about them. They got into trouble for wasting things like apples, and their moms made a lot of their clothes. Every mother I knew had a sewing machine, but they didn't make *all* our dresses the way Beezus's mom always seemed to be doing; they used their sewing machines more for making curtains and tapering jeans. Still, I was probably a lot closer to Henry than I am to you in terms of how many toys I had.

Of course we owned way more stuff than our parents had

owned when they were children. Once we got a box of pears in the mail from Harry & David, and some of them were wrapped in gold foil. Mum said, "You kids can have this foil to play with."

All four of us looked at her. Play with *foil?*

"What should we do with it?" Nelie asked after a second.

"Well, when I was your age," my father said, "I would have wrapped it around my hand and been the Man with the Golden Fist!" He punched the air vigorously.

You could see that both my parents were thinking, "Kids today are spoiled. They don't even know how to appreciate gold foil."

My parents, in turn, owned way more stuff than *their* parents had owned. I'll never forget the way my grandfather and his sister, my great-aunt, reacted when they saw my own kids' playroom with all the dolls and stuffed animals and games and plastic food and action figures lined up on the shelves. They leaned back weakly against each other and burst into helpless laughter. They had grown up poor, and I guess that back in their day, all that kids had to play with was blades of grass. And if you go back a couple of generations in children's books, you'll find Laura Ingalls Wilder using a corncob as a doll. "It wasn't her fault she was a corncob," the narrator says.

My mother's mother, Catherine Smith, with her one doll. She lived in a poor part of Boston then—look at the wrecked-up background.

But Actually, We Were LUCKIER Than You!

I don't want you to feel sorry for us, because owning less stuff and fewer toys meant that we really, really paid attention to the toys we did have. If you have to wait awhile before getting something, getting it at last feels like a solid achievement. Even wanting stuff was fun—well, not exactly fun, but a very *involving* activity. Sometimes, longing for something is more interesting than actually having it. When my son, John, was little and would get a new Ninja Turtle, the first thing he always did was to turn over the package so he could study the Ninja Turtles he *still* wanted—even though the new turtle was sitting in his lap.

And the world's best Engines of Longing were the FAO Schwarz catalog and the Sears catalog.

I know there are catalogs now. All I ever *do* is recycle catalogs. But none of them is anything like the FAO Schwarz and Sears catalogs of my childhood. That's not my opinion; it's just a plain fact. Back then, the FAO Schwarz catalog was ten times bigger than it is now—no, a million times bigger. And the Sears catalog was practically the size of a car. I have a 1965 Sears catalog next to my computer, and it's 1,809 pages long. Of course, a lot of the pages in our Sears catalogs were dedicated to items that only grown-ups cared about, like chain saws and beds and rugs and vacuum cleaners. But there were also pages and pages of toys and clock radios and clothes, as well as interesting photos of girls my age wearing very high, smooth, white underpants. How did they get them to stay so smooth? They looked *ironed*.

The FAO Schwarz catalog was even better, because it had nothing but toys. It came in the fall so parents could order from it for Christmas, and my brother and sisters and I read it over and over, putting hopeful circles around the things we wanted. Next to the old Sears catalog, I also have a 1965 FAO Schwarz catalog. (I got both catalogs from eBay. I'm planning to gradually replace my entire lost childhood with items from eBay.)

Oh, how perfectly I remember everything in it! Especially the skunk puppet on the back page of the catalog. Petunia the Climbing Skunk, she was called, and she cost $12.95. "A most realistic and affectionate pet in the hands of her loving master, ready at all times to obey every command," said the catalog. What kind of command would you give a skunk, I wonder? "Don't spray me"?

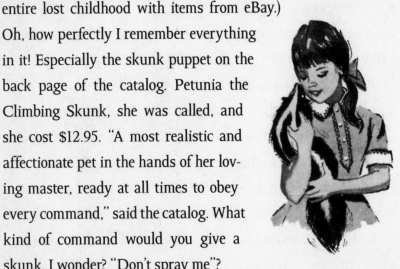

I also longed for Frisky Fox, though he cost seven dollars more. "Quick as lightning are his animated motions as he performs many tricks and capers, limited only by one's imagination. His natural fur body conceals the coil spring which is the secret of the amazingly lifelike actions." The picture of  Frisky Fox showed a rich-looking boy cradling Frisky in his arms as a pack of hunters and hunting dogs rushed toward them. "You're safe now, Frisky," the boy seemed to be saying, though I didn't see how they could get away from men on horseback.

As Christmas drew closer, I would study what I hoped would become my skunk and my fox. Then I would pick up the Sears catalog and pore over the walkie-talkies, which I also wanted. I was always going to get a pair and use them with Robin, the girl who lived two houses down. We were going to talk in our rooms after dark and use them to spy on the big boys who lived down the street and find each other on the playground during recess. . . . Really, with walkie-talkies we could have been completely happy. Except that they wouldn't have worked as well as the catalog promised, so we would have been disappointed—which means it's probably just as well no one ever ended up giving them to us.

That's true as well of several other things I wanted and never got:

★ A Miniature Camera

These were about two inches long, and they took terrible pictures. But who cared? They were *miniature cameras*!

Like many girls back then, I helped out in the office of my middle school. I don't remember what I did. It certainly wasn't anything important like checking up on my classmates' grades or finding out who had detention that day. It was probably chores like putting dittos into a box or Windexing the Formica counter. There was a lost and found box in the office, and naturally I checked it every time I worked there. Usually it held the same things all the time: old scarves, old mittens, and sometimes old buttons. But one morning, there was a miniature camera in the box.

This was like looking into an old bird's nest and finding an emerald. I almost literally couldn't believe what I was seeing. "Look, someone lost a camera," I said to the office lady in a casual voice. "What if no one comes in to get it? Can I have it?"

"We need to leave it there for a month," the office lady answered. "If it's still there after a month, yes—I don't see why you can't take it."

So I waited. No one came for the camera. Two weeks went by, and then three, and then the last week of the month was almost up. And then on the very last day of the month, I came into the office and the camera was gone.

I wanted to spit with rage. I knew, I *knew*, I KNEW that whoever had taken that camera wasn't the real owner. It was another kid who'd been keeping an eye on the lost and found box, just like me. Maybe it was even another girl who worked in the office. That mean pig! Why did *she* deserve it any more than I did? If anyone who's reading this book has a mother who once stole a miniature camera right out from under Ann Hodgman's nose, I want you to make her mail it to me.

On the same subject: my sisters and I all went to the same overnight camp for a few years. The last night of camp was always very dramatic. We would sing sad songs around the campfire, and everyone would be sobbing away—even people like me, who didn't care about camp that much. (Too many activities, not enough time to sit around reading, too many crafts that involved tree bark.) "Don't cry, dear girls," the camp director would say in a sweetly false voice, and that would make us all cry even harder.

Of course the camp director could have had us sing some of the more cheerful camp songs, like "The Prune Song":

No matter how young a prune may be,
he's always full of wrinkles.
A baby prune's just like his dad,
but he's not wrinkled half so bad.

We have wrinkles on our face—
A PRUNE HAS WRINKLES EVERY PLACE!
No matter how young a prune may be,
he's always getting stewed.
Little seed inside the prune,
Is it night or is it noon?
Whatcha doin', pru-in? Stewin'? HUH?

My friends and I liked to sing, "We have wrinkles on our face—A PRUNE HAS WRINKLES ON HIS BUTT!" It was only right and natural. But tonight wasn't the time for "The Prune Song," butts or otherwise. It was the time for "Hang Down Your Head, Tom Dooley" and "Today":

Today, while the blossoms still cling to the vine,
I'll taste your strawberries, I'll drink your sweet wine. . . .

Wait a minute. Wine? For YWCA campers? Maybe it was the sweet wine of memory or something.

"Today" continued on to verses about how "I'll be a dandy, and I'll be a rover" and how "I can't live on promises winter to spring." Where do camps come up with this kind of music? By the end of the campfire, we had practically choked to death on our tears.

After our singing and crying were over, the counselors would pass out paper plates and candles. We'd each light our candle, drip some wax onto our plate, and stick the candles upright in the wax puddles. Then we'd file to the lake, make a wish on our candles, and set the plates on the water. They would drift off into the night, their candles flickering and reflecting on the smooth water.

And God only knows what happened to them afterward, because I bet no one thought of going out in a boat and collecting all that trash the next morning. No, it was about how beautiful they looked as they sailed away into the night—not how much litter they were making. (I *told* you I didn't care about camp that much.)

Anyway, I ran into my younger sister Cathy on the way back to our cabins, and she asked me what I had wished for. "World peace," I said loftily. Cathy looked surprised. "I wished for a camera," she said.

Something else I REALLY, REALLY wanted—this baby raccoon some friends were raising. I wonder what ever happened to him.

★ A SuperBall

These are called high-bounce balls now. They come in all kinds of colors and patterns, and I'm sure *you* have a million of them. You can get glow-in-the-dark high-bounce balls. You can get weirdly shaped high-bounce balls that bounce in unexpected directions, like up into your eye. You can even buy kits to make your own high-bounce balls. You pour some powder into a mold—high-bounce-ium powder, probably—and hold the mold under water. TWO MINUTES LATER, you have a high-bounce ball shaped like the Cat in the Hat. (I'm not going to start calling them high-bounce Cats in the Hat. Let's keep it simple.) Two minutes! When I had to wait for weeks and weeks, it seemed like!

SuperBalls, the original high-bounce balls, were invented in the 1960s by a company called Wham-O. We all owe a lot to Wham-O. They also invented the original Hula Hoop and the original Frisbee and the original Hacky Sack and the original Slip 'N Slide and the original Boogie board and a lot of other cool stuff—the kind of stuff that sweeps through kid culture like a fever. One minute, no one has a Hacky Sack; the next minute, everyone has one, and your school has to make a lot of rules about where you can play with them. Suddenly, your teacher's desk drawers are full of confiscated Hacky Sacks. "You can have them back at the end of the year," the teacher says. And then it's on to the next thing, and the teacher has a lot of leftover Hacky Sacks no one cares about getting back. But it does seem as though a lot of Wham-O's inventions stay popular. I would go on a Slip'n Slide right now, if there were one out in my yard and it weren't 50 degrees and raining outside.

When you're a toy manufacturer, it must be really hard to tell which toys will be a success. I once went to a toy convention where a family was selling something they'd invented called, I think, the Wally Bally. It was a bucket-type thing that you fastened around your waist, and then you fastened a sort of belt-type thing around your waist that had these balls hanging down from the belt, and then you swiveled your hips and jumped up and down to try to make baskets with the balls. Or maybe you held the bucket and it wasn't on a belt. I'm not explaining this very well, but it looked like a lot of fun. The family who had invented it was looking forward to making millions of dollars with it. People at their booth kept wanting to play Wally Bally. And yet who has a Wally Bally now, if that's even the right name?

But SuperBalls were another story. The first SuperBalls bounced into my life in the spring of fourth grade, when a couple of kids suddenly brought them to school. (Of course, the teachers immediately had to make rules about not bouncing them indoors.) These lucky, lucky kids were full of stories about how "the Super-Ball company" had once dropped a giant SuperBall out a skyscraper window. "It has fifty thousand pounds of compressed energy!"—whatever compressed energy was. "When they dropped it out of the skyscraper, and it crushed a convertible, but the ball was in perfect condition!"

Well! Who wouldn't want one after a recommendation like that? I only had to wait for a few days before I had my own, but it seemed like ages. After all, I could have been out with my Super-Ball all that time, not frittering my life away playing Chinese jump rope.

When I finally got my SuperBall, it was so beautiful I could hardly bring myself to play with it. Like all the first SuperBalls, it was a dark blue-purplish gray, totally unlike a typical "toy" color. It had a powdery sheen that was exactly like the bloom on Concord grapes or blueberries. After I'd broken in and given it a bounce or two, the bloom went away—but once it was all off, the SuperBall was shiny all over. It could even be polished for a few days. Then, gradually, it started to get dull and chipped from being bounced on the driveway so many times.

Because that was the thing about SuperBalls: you were never allowed to play with them inside, where they could have stayed smooth. Their bouncing was too crazy and unpredictable. Remember, we had never seen this kind of ball before. You couldn't get a regular rubber ball or a tennis ball to bounce higher than your head and hit the ceiling and come down and careen off at a totally different angle and hit the kitchen bulletin board and knock it down and then hit the cat in the side and then *boing boing boing* away into the hall. The cat would yowl and leap out of the room, and our mothers would order us, "Take that outside right now!" Oh, the wonder of having something like this invented just to *play* with!

I only liked my SuperBall for as long as it stayed smooth. After that, it lost about 65 percent of its appeal for me. But I was stuck with it, because these were the Henry Huggins days. A few years later, mini SuperBalls came out. They were still the same dark bluish color, and they still lost their sheen easily, but at least you could have more of them at once.

★ Band-Aids

When you're a grown-up, it's easy to forget how often kids hurt themselves falling down. About a year ago, I tripped over the gate of my rabbit pen and skinned my knee. Years of knee-skinning anguish rushed back at me in an instant. It really hurts! And I skinned a knee or stubbed a toe at least once a month when I was a kid. From preschool on up, I hoped for a Band-Aid every time I got hurt. Unfortunately, our family rule was that Band-Aids were only administered if we were actually bleeding.

"It looks all right," my dad would say. "You don't need a Band-Aid."

"Oh, good," I would answer, my voice hollow with disappointment. When I was hurting, I wanted some kind of *treatment* for it.

I'm still the same way. Recently I went to the emergency room for X-rays because I was positive my little finger was broken. Next day, the radiologist called me and told me it was fine.

"I *guess* that's good news," I said.

My parents made a Band-Aid exception if my sisters or I skinned our knees hard enough to rip our tights. (Remember, this was back when girls wore dresses to school. In winter, we wore tights with them, because how else could we survive out on the playground?) But other than that, no blood, no Band-Aid. Not even for scrapes that were *killing* us.

This probably made sense in terms of not being wasteful. Besides, I always forgot that every Band-Aid that was put *on* had to be taken *off* at some point. "NO! WAIT! NOT YET!" I would shriek when my parents reached out toward my Band-Aid with their evil claws. Finally they got wise and let me take them off myself, which made things easier because I could stretch out the chore for a couple of days.

The thing is, a Band-Aid makes a sore place feel better even if it's not actually helping it to heal. Maybe a kiss from a parent works on a boo-boo when you're, like, two years old, but after that a Band-Aid's magic is stronger. Band-Aids have that nice plasticky smell and those nice little crisp, supersmooth papers that you peel off. And they look so . . . medical. When my own kids were born, my husband and I decided that we'd always give them Band-Aids—even for scrapes so minor that they were invisible. We also let them use Band-Aids on their toys, with the result that many of Laura's dolls ended up with a Band-Aid coating an inch thick. Laura and her best friend, Emmy, also found many occasions when the stuffed animals needed Band-Aids over their eyes.

Now, though, there are these amazing gel Band-Aids that cost a lot more than regular ones. If Laura and John were still little, I might not let them use those on their toys. But I'd still let them have them on their skin whenever they'd hurt themselves, or thought they had. It's so much fun to watch the gel puff up and turn whitish over a cut!

★ Rose Quartz

Rose quartz is a beautiful pale pink, a clear rose color that, to me, makes it more beautiful than diamonds. I guess it must be possible to find rose quartz in nature; it has to come from somewhere. But I've never seen any except in nature stores and science-museum gift shops.

I used to look at rose quartz on my favorite page of the encyclopedia—the illustration of gems and semiprecious stones. I had a little chip of it in my "mineral collection," which was a flat display I'd gotten as a birthday present once with different kinds of rocks and minerals glued to a sheet of cardboard. Sometimes I wondered about pulling the rose quartz off the cardboard and soaking it to remove the glue so I could hold it and look at it up close. But I always decided it was probably safer on the cardboard.

So when my friend Amy invited me to her family's cabin for the night and told me there was a lot of rose quartz there, I couldn't believe how lucky I was. "Real rose quartz?" I kept asking.

"I swear," said Amy. "My sister and I collect it every time we go there."

For rose quartz that was just lying around waiting to be gathered, I would have gone anywhere. I don't remember anything about the cabin except that we had hamburgers with onions in them for dinner. Onions! Why didn't Amy's mom just dip them in poison while she was at it? But I managed to choke mine down. Getting poisoned was worth it for rose quartz.

So didn't I feel cheated the next morning, when Amy led me to some kind of parking lot and I saw that what she'd been talking about was pinkish *gravel*! And the pieces weren't even solid pink. They were grayish white with little flecks of rusty salmon in them. I hope I managed to hide my disappointment, though I'm afraid it probably seeped through. But maybe a person like Amy, who considered that gravel to be rose quartz, wasn't perceptive enough to notice how I was feeling. I've *still* never found any rose quartz in the wild, and for some reason I also blame Amy for that.

I had an even more disappointing experience one day about a year later, when my friend Priscilla invited me to go see her new bear cub. I didn't know Priscilla very well, and I didn't like going to people's houses after school on the spur of the moment. I liked to plan that kind of thing so I had a few days to know it was coming. But a *bear cub?* Of course I went to her house. If Priscilla had said, "Let's sneak out of school right now," I would have gone.

The bear cub turned out to be a *dog*. A black Newfoundland puppy named, you guessed it, Bear. He was perfectly cute, but he WAS NOT A BEAR CUB. I don't know how I managed to stay at Priscilla's house for a whole afternoon after that.

★ A Geode

Of course I also wanted a geode. Preferably one that was the size of a pineapple. I liked to imagine walking around in—where? the desert? a forest? a dry riverbed?—with my friends. Suddenly, I would say, "Look at that rock."

"Why?" my friends would answer. "It's just a boring, unimportant rock. Let's ignore it."

"Not so fast," I'd say solemnly. "There's something about *that* rock. I think we should take it home with us."

"What?" my friends would sputter. "Lug home that big heavy thing? There's no point. *You* carry it, if you think it's so great."

So I would carry the rock home, and when I got it home, I'd find someone to open it for me. (As with its location, the way you "opened" a rock was also vague to me. Did people saw rocks open, or use an ax on them, or what?) And once it was opened, it would reveal itself as a geode: two cavelike rock halves each lined with a lustrous, sparkling bed of amethyst crystals.

I wouldn't have to share my geode halves, of course. They were my prize for carrying the geode all the way home by myself.

Come to think of it, I believe that that dry riverbed or forest floor also contains a bunch of arrowheads! I can't wait to really find it someday.

★ An Electric Guitar

Actually, I didn't want one of these, though I liked reading about them in the Sears catalog. But as a boy, my husband, David, wanted an electric guitar desperately. His friend Ralph Lewis had an electric guitar, but David's parents didn't seem to understand that David would die without one. So David decided to come up with a surefire way to convince them. He borrowed Ralph's guitar and amplifier, took them home, and set them up outside the front door of his house. He put on a nylon jacket that he imagined looked like leather and combed his bangs down over his eyes so he'd look more like the Beatles. Then he picked up the guitar and rang the front doorbell. When his mom answered the door, David started whaling away on the guitar. He didn't know how to play, of course—or, as I'm sure he thought, he didn't know how to play *yet*. But wouldn't the first glimpse of his coolness cause his mother to change her mind instantly?

I'll let you guess the answer to that.

Birthday Parties

Once I'm sitting down, I'm hard to dislodge. If I'm at my computer, I'll sometimes Google something for an hour rather than walk two steps away from my desk to find the book that has the fact I need. I like to stay put, especially if I have a book with me. Often when I'd go on picnics with my family as a child, I would just stay in the car reading while everyone else swam and walked around and did other picnic stuff.

I'm also hard to lure out of the house. When I'm invited somewhere, I usually have a great time after I'm actually there—but I spend the whole day before the event dreading it. I even start to get mad at whoever has invited me over. Don't they *know* how stressful it is for me to have fun? Why does everyone always want to be flapping around instead of staying comfortably on their own sofas? Why do people insist on visiting each other in person instead of just talking on the phone or e-mailing? And why didn't they give me more warning—like six months—so I could prepare myself?

One party I liked was my own first birthday. I got to wear a hundred-year-old dress and do whatever I wanted to my birthday cake.

When my son, John, was two, he was invited to the birthday party of a little girl named Jaime. The instant he woke up from his nap on the day of the party, John said excitedly, "Time go Gamey buhbuh pahty?"

I was not one bit like that as a kid. My friend Suzy Wilkinson's birthday party was typical: I spent the week before it wishing I didn't have to go. Suzy's parents were taking us to see the movie *Savage Sam*. I strongly doubted whether I'd be able to get through it, but Suzy reassured me.

"It's about a dog!" she said. "You love dogs!"

True, but I wasn't sure I loved movies about big rangy hunting dogs with tough-sounding names like Savage Sam. It turned out, though, that Savage Sam himself was the least of my problems. I was in second grade, and I had only seen two movies before: *Hey There, It's Yogi Bear!* and *Mary Poppins*. ("*Mary Poppins* is better than the Yogi Bear movie," I said to my father when we were coming out of the theater. "I don't know about that," Dad replied. "I think the Yogi Bear movie was more honest." I had no idea what he meant.) Neither of them was good preparation for *Savage Sam*, in which some pioneer children who had been LEFT ALONE BY THEIR PARENTS were kidnapped by mean Apaches.

Even worse, from my point of view, was the fact that the Apaches were mean to Savage Sam. He might be savage, but he was a dog, and I couldn't stand watching anyone hurt a dog. The instant I realized what was going to happen, I was out in the lobby crying—and I spent the rest of the movie there. I hovered over by the popcorn, fearfully peeking into the theater once in a while. Mrs. Wilkinson came out to check on me every few minutes, but I refused to go back in.

"It's just a *movie*," she said. She sounded frustrated and cranky, and can you blame her? A whole grown-up was being wasted on one party guest, and birthday parties are already hard enough for parents.

"I know," I wanted to answer, "but things like that really did happen, so what's the point of saying it's pretend?" That wasn't the kind of thing you could explain to an adult, but it still makes perfect sense to me.

I'm glad to say that my daughter, Laura, has inherited the same attitude. When Laura first saw *E.T.*—she was four, which was awfully young—she liked it, but in bed that night she worried that E.T. would come into her room. David tried the "it's just a movie" line. Laura wasn't impressed. "Yes, but I'm sure it's realistic in some ways," she said. Then she heard a plane flying overhead and asked if it was a flying saucer. The part of the movie that bothered her most was where E.T. turns up in that river all cold and gray. Laura said, "I'm glad that when I die I'll just die and not fall in a river like that." She added, "I wish I'd had glasses to keep me from seeing that part of the movie."

Bowling Was Even Worse

Movies were a bad birthday party activity unless someone could swear to me ahead of time that animals wouldn't be hurt. But bowling—oh, no, no, no, no, no. There was no way to promise me anything good about bowling birthday parties.

Bowling alleys were like dimly lit, low-ceilinged, evil planets. There were those ugly shoes we had to put on, first of all. *Tie* shoes at a *party*, when we could have been wearing beautiful party shoes. And all those grown-ups walking around in clothes I didn't understand (bowling shirts, I mean), and the thundery rumble the balls made rolling down the lanes, and the bone-breaking sound the pins made as they fell, and then the way the balls mysteriously reappeared in those whatever-they-were-calleds, those ball-holding machines . . . and this was fun? This was something people *chose* to do? I knew I would be hopeless at the game itself, so I didn't bother trying. When it was my turn, I would listlessly pad up in my ugly shoes and, basically, drop the ball into the gutter. Sometimes I used so little energy that the ball didn't even roll, and I would have to give it a push.

What fun I must have been for the birthday girl! But in fairness to myself, I had *tried* to get out of the party; it was just that my mother wouldn't let me stay home. She made me go to miniature-golf birthday parties, too. "Tell her I can't come," I once begged her when I opened an invitation to a miniature-golf party. "Tell her it's against our religion." That's what I always told other girls if they wanted to play any card game harder than Crazy Eights. "Cards are against my religion," I would say regretfully. I knew no one could argue with that.

But as far as I can remember, I was never allowed to get out of a birthday party. Not for religious reasons, not for any reasons. Maybe if I had thrown up on the way out of the house I could have stayed home, but unfortunately that never happened.

Me and my friends at my eighth birthday party. Look how dressed up we always got for parties! My friend Muffy, with the long hair, is at the end on the left. I'm next to her. If you look really closely, you might be able to tell that we were wearing identical dresses.

So What Kind of Parties DID You Like, Ann?

I liked birthday parties to be safely inside or, at the very most adventurous, out in the yard for relay races. (Relay races were okay with me because the outcome didn't depend on one person.) My own birthday parties always began with a game of Spiderweb, which my parents would have set up earlier that day. We'd each get a card with our name on it, attached to a long, long string. The strings were wound all around the living room—in and out of the furniture, under the piano, twisted up with other strings—and we each had to untangle our own string to get to our prizes.

Once the living room was clear of strings, it was time for the Kim's Game, which I'm sure you've played at some point. My mother would bring in a tray filled with twenty little objects. A jack, say, and a fork, and a toy soldier, and an apple, and—get it? Little objects. Then she would cover the tray and take it away, and we'd each write down as many of the objects as we could remember.

Then, as long as we already had pens and paper, we'd play that game where you try to make as many little words out of one big word as you can. When I was in fourth grade, I remember, the word was "Washington." As soon as my mom went out of the room to set the timer, Mindy Perlman said, "Are swear words allowed?" And we all realized that, yes, there was one big, obvious swear word in there. I was the birthday girl, so I said it was allowed.

I got into sort-of trouble at Cindy Turner's birthday party. We were playing another good kind of game—a homemade version of the *excellent* Scattergories, which you should get if you don't have it already. (Ask for it for your birthday!) Mrs. Turner gave us the categories. One category was birds, and I put down "titmouse" for the letter *T*.

"*Titmouse?*" said Mrs. Turner.

"It's a kind of bird," I said defensively. And it is. It's a sparrow-sized gray bird with a crest on its head. I had seen them at our bird feeder lots of times.

Mrs. Turner allowed me the point, but I could see that she was bothered. Later, when Cindy's father came into the room, Mrs. Turner said quietly to him, "Did you know there was a bird called a titmouse?"

At the birthday table (oh, and that was another nonfun thing about me—I didn't really like cake or ice cream), we always tried to get a game of Telephone going—you know, the one where you whisper something into the ear of the person next to you, and they whisper it into the ear of the person next to them, and so on, and by the time it gets to the end of the line it's HiLaRiOuSlY scrambled up. Or at least that's the theory of the game. In practice, either you heard much too clearly and had to make something up when it was your turn to pass the phrase along, or you couldn't hear it at all and had to make up a *different* something. So that made two kinds of pretending already, plus the pretend laughter you had to give when the last person in the line said something impossible like "Door pear elephant shoes? No, really, that's what I thought it *was!*"

I Turn Out to Be a Bad Slumber Partier

In fourth grade, lots of girls started switching over to slumber parties. The first one I went to was at Kathy Durkin's house, and I was very surprised when, just before *The Man from U.N.C.L.E.* came on TV, Kathy grabbed a comb and started passing it around. "We have to comb our hair for Illya," she said.

"Illya? What's that?" I asked.

"Illya Kuryakin! The cute guy on the show!"

"Oh, *him*," I said. I had never seen *The Man from U.N.C.L.E.* I combed my hair like everyone else, though. After the show, when we pretended to be in an old silent movie by switching a flashlight on and off and jumping around, I also acted as if I knew what everyone else was doing. But when it started to get late, I rebelled.

At about midnight, my friends and I suddenly discovered that I was the type of slumber-party guest who says, "Come on, guys. Isn't it time we got some shut-eye?" I said "shut-eye" in a joky voice, as if I really didn't care much whether we went to sleep or not. But I cared. Oh, I cared. I don't know why I was so worried; it wasn't as if I had to go to work in the morning. But somehow I couldn't bear the thought of being tired the next day.

Since no one (including me) was actually sleepy, no one paid attention to me. As the night went on, though, they started to get mad. Meanwhile, *I* was getting frantic. Now it was two A.M. If we woke up at eight, we would only have had six hours of sleep. And now it was three A.M. . . . and now it was almost light out! We were *never* going to get enough sleep!

Finally I announced, "I don't care what you do. *I'm* going to sleep now."

I doubt that the other girls cared what I did by that point. All I'd been contributing to the fun for three hours was complaints about how late it was getting. When I woke up the next morning, I saw that they had gotten so sick of me that they'd moved their sleeping bags way, way across to the other side of the room.

And I had plenty of time to brood about this, because I woke up way before everyone else. What was I supposed to do now, I wondered. Just lie there quietly? I hadn't brought a book, and all the books in the Durkins' den were boring grown-up ones like *The Agony and the Ecstasy* and *Hawaii.*

I cleared my throat a few times, hoping one of the other girls would wake up naturally. *"Hey, you guys!"* I whispered piercingly. Again, no luck. I just had to lie there and bounce around in my sleeping bag until someone else woke up.

I *did* like being scared at slumber parties. It was creepily fun when it started to get dark and a girl would suddenly gasp, "I just saw someone looking in the window!"

"You did not," another girl would say. "You're making it up." (And she was—or, to put it kindly, her imagination was.)

"No, I swear! It was a face! Looking in! There's someone out there!"

We would press our faces against the windows and stare out at the shrubbery in the backyard.

"See? *There!*"

"I don't see anything," someone would say. "What did he look like?"

"He was low to the ground. Hunched over and scrambling along."

"Like a monkey, you mean?"

"It was probably a dog," someone said boredly. "Anyway, you said he was looking in the *window* before."

"He was! He scrambled up to the window, and—LOOK, I THINK THAT'S HIM AGAIN!"

A volley of screams rose up like a wall, and the mom of the house came rushing in. "Girls, for the love of God," she said crossly. "You almost gave me a heart attack."

And séances. Those were fun, too, partly because half the girls took them seriously and the other half thought they were a total joke. We would turn out the lights and gather in a circle around some kind of table, in case the spirit we were summoning decided to rap on the tabletop when he arrived. Then we would join hands and put on mystical expressions. The most experienced-at-séances girl would take charge. At one party, I remember, we summoned the spirit of George Washington, and the girl in charge was Cammy Whitman.

"George . . . George . . . ," said Cammy in a low, spooky voice.

"Don't call him George!" Barb Alden interrupted, shocked. "He was our *president*!"

"All right, all right. Start over," said Cammy. "George Washington . . . George Washington . . . do you hear us, George?"

"Washington," added Barb.

Silence. We all looked around.

"We are trying to seek you," said a girl who didn't go to our school. I thought to myself that you don't *try* to seek someone; you just *seek* him. But I didn't say it aloud. I was half-believing that something might happen, and I didn't want to wreck things.

More silence.

"Our country is at war," intoned Cammy. "Come to our aid."

"Come back and see what a mess everything is," said Betsy Prior in a normal voice. Cammy frowned at her. Cammy's parents were Republicans, and Betsy's were Democrats.

Still, silence.

"I think I heard something," whispered Miriam Schulman after a second.

"That was my stomach," said Barb, and we all burst out laughing, except for Cammy.

Séances always ended that way.

The Scavenger Hunt

In sixth grade, my friend Debby Gladstein had the first scavenger-hunt birthday party. Mrs. Gladstein divided us into teams of four. Each team was given a list of stuff to look for and the name of the street where we could go door-to-door. (You couldn't trespass on another team's street.) It was a cold January afternoon, and as we raced off into the rapidly darkening street, Sari Adams said, "Dee's good at English accents. Dee, talk in an English accent at the houses."

This seemed like the perfect way around having to talk to strangers. None of the rest of the team would have to do it, and if people thought Dee was English—well, then, maybe they would think *we* were English too!

So when we got to the first house, Dee stood in front while the rest of us cowered behind her. Dee rang the bell, and a lady came to the door.

It's not possible to give you a real idea of what Dee sounded like, but I'll do my best. What came out of her mouth was, roughly, "Dah yah hef any of ziss sings in yah hoos?"

"Excuse me?" said the lady.

After that, Dee wouldn't use her accent anymore, and she made us take turns asking for the stuff on our list.

Olden-Days Presents

We didn't give our friends birthday presents when I was a girl. Just a hug was enough when the birthday girl greeted you at the door.

Are you *crazy*? Of course we gave presents. We weren't like the boys in my son John's class, who—after about third grade—just started giving one another money. (A lot of the parents I know thought this was shocking, but I have to say it sure made things easier for parents, besides giving the birthday boy something you *knew* he wanted.)

Some of the most popular presents my friends and I gave were:

★ Breyer Colts

A whole Breyer horse was too expensive to give as a present, but a colt was fine. "I already have this one," I remarked politely when I got a Breyer colt at my seventh birthday party.

"Now you can pretend you have twins!" said my mother brightly. But I really couldn't. Even identical twin colts wouldn't stand in the same exact positions.

★ China Animals

That's what we called them, anyway. I see that online they're now called "animal figurines." I don't like that name, but I hate the name "porcelain pets" even more. There was a bookstore in our town that had the best collection of china animals. They were tiny—the biggest ones were less than three inches long—but very realistic. My mother still has all hers from when she was a girl, I still have all mine, Laura still has all hers, and the bookstore in the town where I live now still sells the same kind. The best one I ever got was a pond with little ripple marks on it and three ducks to set inside the ripples—a mother, a yellow duckling, and a half duckling with its legs paddling in the air. The front half was supposed to be underwater, you see.

If a girl had a specific breed of dog or color of cat, she usually ended up getting more than one china animal that looked like her pet. But since they were breakable, it wasn't so bad to have an extra in stock.

★ Autograph Books

I still have mine; it's in my living room. Let's take a look! Here it is. It's red leatherine with gold writing on the cover, and the pages are all different colors. The black pages must have been a challenge when I was young, since we didn't have gel pens then.

My friends' autographs are not like the ones Laura Ingalls Wilder's friends wrote in her autograph book in *Little Town on the Prairie*. For instance, Ida Brown wrote, "In memory's golden casket, drop one pearl for me." Here's my friend Candy's autograph:

> Violets are blue,
> Roses are red,
> Sugar is lumpy
> And so is your HEAD!!

Her brother just signed his name in a flourishing scrawl. Boys weren't supposed to write poems or jokes or anything, I guess.

Then there's

Sometimes I'm naughty
Sometimes I'm nice
But now I'll be naughty and sign my name twice!
—Kathy Yurman
—Kathy Yurman

Eva Patry wrote

God made rivers
God made lakes
God made you
But we all make mistakes!
2 in a car
2 little kisses
2 weeks later
Mr. and Mrs.!

Karen Liebmann folded over a corner on her page and wrote on the flap, "For dirty people only!" When you lifted the flap, you saw the word SOAP.

Judy Munter wrote

If your troubles are many,
And your rewards are few,
Remember the mighty oak
Was once a nut like you.

YY ["too wise"] U R YY U B I C U R YY 4 me.
I N V U 4 U R A Q T.

My favorite signature is my friend Debby Gladstein's. She wrote in Elmer's Glue and, when it dried, outlined the words in pen. And what she wrote was:

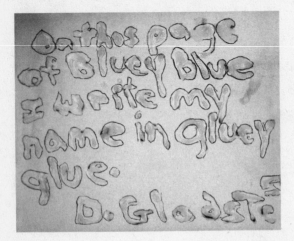

Here's what it says, in case you can't read it: "On this page of Bluey Blue, I write my name in gluey glue."

. . . And I just found out *now* that my husband must have gotten his hands on this book at some point. On one page, in his regular grown-up handwriting, it says, "In the future, I will marry you." The funny thing is that as I was reading it, my heart started to race a little bit. I thought, "A boy back then liked me! Who was it?" I couldn't help being disappointed when I saw "David Owen." Not that I don't love him and everything, but it was so exciting for a second there to think that a boy back in fifth grade wanted to *marry* me. If only it had been Bruce Kline!

★ Underpants

I actually went to one birthday party where a guest had brought underpants as a present. (We never called them "panties.") Just plain, white high-waisted Carter's underpants, the kind we all wore—two three-packs of them. We couldn't help snickering when the birthday girl opened them. "They'll come in handy," the girl who had brought them said in a weak voice.

I wondered if maybe her mother wasn't as well organized as mine was about presents. If Mum spotted something that would make a good birthday present—little silk embroidered Japanese purses, or a good new type of china animal, she bought it in multiples and stashed them away. Maybe this girl's mother had suddenly realized just before the party that she didn't have a present on hand and had just grabbed some unopened underpants from a shelf.

I hope that was it, anyway. Because the thought of a mom who would *shop* for underpants as a present is too sad. If only I had been allowed to skip that party, think how much happier we'd ALL be now!

Names

When my daughter, Laura, was three, she began calling her father Dave instead of Dad. Lots of kids experiment with using their parents' first names, and David was delighted by it. He especially liked the idea of Laura's parents being "Mommy and Dave."

"It makes me sound like your young boyfriend," he told me.

Of course John grew up hearing his big sister call their father Dave, so he did it too. Once, when John was also about three, he told David, "I'm going to write a book called *Daves These Days.* The first sentence will be, 'These days, Daves are bad.'"

But back to Laura. As soon as she had gotten the Dave thing

established, she began trying to call me Ann. I didn't like that, though. I told her, "I think people should be called what they want to be called, and I want to be called Mommy."

Laura thought for a while, and she said, "Then I want to be called Megan."

I couldn't see any way out of this, so I did start calling her Megan. I worked it into every sentence.

"Megan, it's time for lunch, Megan."

"What kind of sandwich do you want, Megan?"

After half an hour of this, "Megan" said, "I guess I want to be Laura again."

It's funny, the names kids like. At three, I thought the most beautiful name in the world was Matilda. That was because some friends of my parents had a dog, a boxer, named Matilda. Now, looking back through the mists of time, I can't see my way to understanding how *any* name attached to *any* dog could have struck me as beautiful. In later years, Roald Dahl's book *Matilda* might have been a reasonable inspiration—but a dog? A boxer, especially, with its big square head? But I was so in love with the name that I begged my parents to name my new baby sister Matilda. They wouldn't do it. They named her Cornelia instead.

By the time the next baby came along, I had outgrown the name Matilda—which is just as well, because the next baby was a boy. Now I was in love with all the Christine-type names. This came along partly because I had a good friend named Christy.

All I remember about Christy now is her name and the fact that when I was five and was having lunch at her house, she held out her cupped hands and said, "Look, a bowl! Pour your milk into it." I did. Christy's mom scolded me, and I feebly said, "But she *told* me to!" I realized right away that that's one excuse you just can't get away with.

Christy, Christine, Christina, Kristin, Kirsten . . . all those names seemed as beautiful as flowers when I was in second grade. My favorite Christmas present that year (hey, Christmas would be a good name, too!) was a baby doll dressed in a christening gown (hey, Christening would be a—no, I guess it wouldn't) and lying on a lace pillow. If you wound up the music box in her stomach, a tinkly song—accompanied by a grinding noise from the machinery—would play while the doll's head slowly moved back and forth on the pillow. It sounds a little creepy now. A music-box *baby*? But oh, how I loved that doll.

She had to have the perfect name, obviously. Her first name couldn't be anything but Christy. But what about the last name? Finally I hit on the perfect choice.

"You remember how President Kennedy was shot in the fall?" I asked my mother. Of course she remembered; it had been the biggest news story in the world. "Well, I'm going to name my doll Christy Kennedy," I went on.

"That's a *beautiful* name," said my mom kindly.

It was not only beautiful, I thought—it was a fitting way to remember our late president. I thought maybe I should write a letter to his family to tell them about it and cheer them up.

Right around the same time, I also had a toy dog named Leprosy. Leprosy—pronounced LEP-ro-see—is a disease, but I didn't know that. I thought the name was pronounced LEP-rosy, and it made me think of a beautiful rosy perfume. I also had, and still have, a tiny teddy bear named Girl-Ted, even though he's a boy. I got him (and named him) when I was three, and I want to be buried with him when I die. A few years ago I bought Girl-Ted a tiny purple wife. Her name, of course, is Boy-Ted. I don't care what happens to Boy-Ted when I die; she's just company for Girl-Ted. You can have her if you want.

Leprosy, Girl-Ted, and Girl-Ted's unimportant wife, Boy-Ted.

In third grade, I discovered that you could end a name with "belle." Sarabelle, Annabelle—they were nice enough, but wouldn't the name Christabelle be extra-super-fantastically beautiful? Of course it would. I decided that my first child would be named Christabelle. (Not if it was a boy, of course.)

Picking Names for My Future Kids

My friends and I were very into choosing names for our future children. I bet you are too. I bet you've also decided how many children you'll have, and whether they'll be boys or girls, and so on. For a while when she was little, my daughter planned to have twelve children—all six months apart. One of them was going to be named Hannah, and another was going to be Dylan. That's all Laura can remember now, but you know how it is when you have twelve kids. You're so busy that it's hard to keep track of things.

There were two directions you could go in when you named your future children. You could make a list of all the favorite names you'd ever had, including a few that you'd made up. Thinking about those lists reminds me of the time I raided my sister Cathy's diary (it was in the second drawer of her bureau) and saw that she had written, "One day my children will be reading this. So HI! to you guys."

You could also name your children after your best friends—or people you wanted to be your best friends.

A girl I admired tremendously in third, fourth, and fifth grade was Mindy Perlman. Mindy Perlman had *everything*. She was smart, she was good at sports, she had a new baby sister, and she kept a list of all her friends, ranked in order of preference, in a little notebook in her desk.

"You're third on my list," she told me once. I was proud. Many of Mindy's friends were so much cooler than I that they called her Pindy Merlman instead of Mindy Perlman. Maybe now I'd get to do the same thing!

Unfortunately, later that same day, Mindy said, "I'm sorry, but I remembered some other people. I had to move you down to seventh place."

"At least I'm still in the top ten," I thought humbly.

Once, in fourth grade, we had to draw wedges of watermelon to decorate the top of the blackboard. It was one of those "seasonal" projects that our art teacher, Miss Stinkyface (that was her actual, real name), was very big on. Cartoony turkeys wearing Pilgrim hats at Thanksgiving, a pile of wrapped presents at Christmas, a rippling flag for Flag Day—those were the kinds of things Miss Stinkyface had us make with the crayons we kept in our desks. In addition to many other bad qualities—she once yanked a boy in my class out of his chair by his ears—Miss Stinkyface liked all our art projects to be identical. I guess she thought that would make them more decorative when they were lined up over the blackboard. Well, it wasn't hard to copy her watermelon picture—except that when all the wedges had been tacked up around the blackboard, we noticed that one of them had green flesh and a red rind.

A backward piece of watermelon! Hah hah hah hah hah hah hah! We didn't get much to laugh about in art class, so we jumped at the chance now. "Who did that one? Who did that one?" we all asked, twisting and squealing at our desks. But no one would fess up. And can you blame them?

Later, though, Mindy came up to me and whispered, "Ann, I have to tell you something. *I* made that watermelon! I just forgot what watermelons look like!"

Perfect Pindy Merlman had made a backward watermelon? I could hardly believe it. In fact, I still can't quite believe it. How hard is it to remember what a watermelon looks like? But I was honored that she had confided in me.

She still didn't move me back to third place in her best friend list, though.

Nicknames

Which reminds me of something terrible. When my kids were little, they had a tape with a song on it called "I Hate My Name." The chorus went like this:

I hate my name, oh, I hate my name,
I'm gonna throw it in the Atlantic Ocean!
I hate my name, oh, I hate my name,
I'm gonna throw it away.

That's all I remember—that, and the fact that my husband said the singer on the tape sounded as though he was lying on his back with his mouth drooping open while he sang. "Some of the people who make children's tapes are the lowest form of life on the planet," David said. Anyway, we played that tape a lot in the car, and the song got lodged in my brain. One day, as I was going down to the basement to get some bread from the freezer, I lustily began to sing it aloud. (If you know me, you know that whenever I sing, I'm about to get in trouble.) The words I bellowed out were:

I hate my name, oh, I hate my name,
I'm gonna throw it in the Atlantic Ocean!
I hate my name, oh, I hate my name—
Oh. Hi, Emmett.

I hadn't realized that our housepainter was working in the basement.

There was no way he could have missed my singing—I was mooing like a cow—so I had to pretend I didn't care. I kept on singing, but more quietly, as if I were preoccupied while searching for the bread in the freezer. Then I kind of drifted off into whistling the same tune. Finally, I said, "Oh, here it is," and grabbed the bread and ran upstairs.

Emmett never mentioned this little adventure. But then he wouldn't, would he?

Actually, I don't hate my name and want to throw it in the Atlantic Ocean. I think Ann is an okay name. Maybe a little plain—it would be nice to have a name that was more than three letters long—but I don't have any problems with it. I like my middle name, too. Now I do, at least. It's Hampton (which was my great-grandfather's last name), and when I was a kid I *would* have thrown it in the Atlantic Ocean if I could have.

"Hampton" always made me think of ham, and of laundry hampers; it also sounded sort of fat to me, for some reason. I envied kids who had regular, first-name names for their middle names, and I vowed to give my own children ordinary middle names. But then when I grew up, I broke my promise. Laura's middle name is Hazard; John's is Bailey. They've had their share of hating their middle names, but I think they're used to them now.

There was one big problem with the name Ann, though. When teachers yell at a class, they have a way of yelling "and" at the beginning of their sentences. Well, maybe you don't know anything about this because maybe teachers never yell nowadays. What I mean is, a teacher (let's say it's my old art teacher, Miss Stinkyface, again) might say, "I have never seen a class behave so badly. You are disrespectful and unruly. AND when I get my claws on your ears, I will rip them off your head."

Like that.

If your name is Ann and the teacher suddenly bellows out "AND," you always think she's about to yell specifically at you. It's very startling. I would bolt up in my seat, then sag back with relief when I realized that Miss Stinkyface wasn't actually talking to me.

If I had a nickname, I used to think, *life would be so much easier!* I suppose I could have been called Annie, but I hated that nickname. It made me think of the comic strip Little Orphan Annie, with her big empty eyes, and of Annie Oakley, with her stupid guns and her fringed cowgirl skirt. Even more, I hated Hampton Schnoz, which was what some of the boys in my fourth-grade class called me. They called me that because of my horrible, horrible middle name and because everyone in the class said my nose was too big.

I myself had never noticed the nose problem until I was at a friend's house one afternoon. This was my friend Kathy Durkin, who was allowed to watch *The Man from U.N.C.L.E.* Kathy had *everything* at her house. She had a trampoline and a poodle and an ice-cream-making kit and a Sno-Kone kit and a kit where you made beautiful flowers out of tissue paper and all the junk food you could eat, and she was allowed to stay up late, and she only lived a block from our school, so the class picnics were always at her house. (Council Rock Elementary School, our school was called, and there were some big paintings of Native Americans in the lobby. I wonder if they're still there.) Kathy also had a very cute older brother, who I was half-scared of and half had a crush on. If he was in the house, my invisible antennae were always tuned to him.

Anyway, one afternoon Kathy and I were weaving some pot holders on her little pot-holder loom when she suddenly looked searchingly at me and said, "No offense, Ann, but you have kind of a big nose."

That was the first time I'd ever thought about my nose at all. It was also the first time I realized that whenever someone starts a sentence with the words "no offense, but . . . ," whatever they say *will* be offensive. Pay attention to this, because it's true! If anyone you know says "No offense, but . . . ," that person is about to insult you in some way. (Also, if anyone ever says "with all due respect . . . ," they're about to disagree with you.) I don't think Kathy meant to be mean. I think she honestly believed she was doing me a favor. Sort of like "Ann's been walking all over Planet Earth like a person with a normal nose. *Someone's* got to tell her she's making a mistake."

Once someone has pointed out the size of your nose, you don't stop thinking about it. When I got home, I kept looking at my reflection in the mirror, trying to catch a glimpse of myself from the side. My nose did look kind of beaky, didn't it? And did it droop at the end, too? Oh, why had I had to find this out? My whole life was ruined! But maybe it was better to know the truth. Since I was going to have to start acting like a person with a terrible flaw, I should be grateful to Kathy for helping me understand reality.

The problem might have gone away if I hadn't dumbly asked my friend David Lee, who lived the next street over—and who happened to be in my class—if *he* thought my nose was too big. I guess I was imagining that he'd say, "No, of course not! It's just right! You're really very cute. In fact, I like you. And I mean I *like* like you."

WHAT WAS *WRONG* WITH ME?

You don't ask a fourth-grade boy if your nose is too big and expect him to be *nice* about it! Of course David started making fun of my nose—"that schnoz of yours," he called it—and of course he told his friends about it, and one thing led to another, and before I knew it I was Hampton Schnoz for the rest of the year.

I don't have to tell you that *that* wasn't the kind of nickname I wanted. What's embarrassing now is that the nickname I did want was even kind of worse:

Twink.

Yes, Twink.

A girl named Twink seemed to me like just the kind of girl I wanted to be—perky and smiley and never shy or awkward.

Twink would have her hair in a blond pageboy, which was my favorite hairstyle to draw when I was a kid. (It was the opposite of my own hair, which flipped out in all directions like a pile of dead leaves.) Also, she would be good at sports—always picked first for teams—and would be able to do a cartwheel just like *that*. (When I even tried doing a somersault, I was as clumsy as a lobster.) When she walked into a room, people's faces would brighten, which is part of how Twink would have earned her name. Twink would seem to twinkle like a star, shedding light on everything around her. *She* would never have a big schnoz.

How to *become* Twink was the problem. You can't just tell your class to switch you from Hampton Schnoz. . . . I figured that my best bet would be to change my name at camp that summer.

After all, isn't camp the place for nicknames? My mother-in-law, whose last name was Matz, tried to get her named changed to Matzie at camp. And no one calls camp counselors by their real names. In fact, when I was a first-grader in my first day camp, we got to choose our counselors' names. I suggested Weasel for our counselor Nancy, and I couldn't understand why she seemed upset with me. Weren't weasels perfectly nice animals? Smart, quick, good predators, with valuable fur used to trim kings' robes—what was the problem?

But back to Twink and my fifth-grade overnight camp. When the counselors in our cabin did the roll call on the first day and got to Ann Hodgman, I planned just to smile and say, "People actually call me Twink."

"Twink!" the counselors would say. "What a darling name!" And the girls in my cabin would unanimously elect me cabin leader.

By the time I got back to school in sixth grade, my new life would be all set. I'd be able to tell everyone, "All the kids at camp started calling me Twink, for some reason."

"Twink!" my friends would say. *"Why?"*

I would smile and look down modestly. "I don't know. Something about my personality, I guess."

Maybe it would have worked. Maybe. But as it turned out, there were two girls in my cabin at camp who were also fifth-graders at my school. They certainly knew that no one called me Twink.

Instead, the girls in the cabin started calling me Hodgie. I didn't like that nearly as much as Twink, but at least it was better than Hampton Schnoz. People still call me Hodgie sometimes. A few years ago, one of my best friends started calling me Franny, and then it changed to Fanny and then Fancini. In return, I call her Marph. Marph's brother Jim, who is also a friend of mine, calls me Fatty.

By the way, when I grew up, I asked a plastic surgeon if she thought my nose was too big, and she said yes. But I'm going to leave it the way it is.

First Days of School

I was *not* looking forward to my first day of kindergarten.

Do you remember your first day of school this year? Well, of course you do. For you, it was probably, like, two minutes ago. For me, it's ninety bazillion years ago, and yet I remember all the first days of school as clearly as . . . as clearly as if they were only *fifty* bazillion years ago.

You look around the classroom and think, "*This* is my

class? *These* are the kids I have to be friends with this year?" You go home and tell your parents that your class has all the bad kids. And then, by the end of the year, you can't imagine ever being in another class. On the

first day of school the next year, you look around the classroom and think, "*This* is my class? Last year's class was way better."

Also, you look at the kids a grade behind you and can't believe how young and little they look. Did you look that young last year? Impossible! But you must have! Well, never mind. *This* year, you're as big and old as anyone could possibly get. And then the following year, you think the same things again.

Meanwhile, your teacher is wishing he had spent ten minutes the night before working on the pronunciation of any of the unusual names in the class. Instead, he stumbles on several of them when he calls the roll.

"Brian Sut-hit—Soothy—uh . . ."

"Suthithamrongsawat," supplies Brian, wishing everyone were dead.

"That's a tongue twister!" says the teacher. But it wouldn't have been if he'd just done a little homework and written the names phonetically. Kids like to have their names pronounced right on the first day of school.

Miss Streeter and Mrs. Mills

My first day of kindergarten, and all the rest of my days of kindergarten, was at an old, old Rochester school called Public School 47—PS 47, we said. PS 47 was a square, two-story, dark brick building in the center of an absolutely flat lot with nothing else on it. It was about three blocks from where I lived in University Park, and on the first morning, I walked there with my mom and my friend Benjy Sax and *his* mom. My dad took a picture of us before we left. I was wearing a pink-and-white striped dress and looking sadly away into the bushes. Benjy was wearing striped shorts and a white polo shirt and staring boldly at the camera. Benjy was always very brave. Our fathers were residents together at the same medical school, where there were lots of parties. When Benjy met our dads' boss, he stuck his finger waaaaaaaaay up his nose before he said hi.

Come to think of it, I wasn't all that shy at hospital parties either. I loved the hospital, because it was where my dad worked. (I still love hospitals and am always happy when I get to go to one.) When I was four, I got a new petticoat that I was very proud of. It was starchy and lacy and was supposed to help puff up the skirt of your party dress, and I thought it made me look like an old-fashioned girl in a book. So when my dad introduced me to some other doctor at a hospital party, I shouted, "I just got a new petticoat!" and whisked my skirt up around my head so the doctor could see.

I'm sure my parents were embarrassed, but nowhere near as embarrassed as some friends of theirs were at another hospital party—this one outside, in the summer. The two-year-old daughter of those friends was walking around on a hospital tennis court when she suddenly shouted, "Mama! I have to GO!" Then she pulled down her pants, squatted, and pooped on the tennis court. "I had to pick it up in a *cocktail napkin*," her mortified mother told my mother later.

I also liked to wear just my petticoat outside, sometimes with a sweater if it was cold out. My parents have a picture of me,

Me in my beloved petticoat, with my beloved bow and arrow.

barefoot, wearing my petticoat and a red sweater and shooting a bow and arrow toward the camera. The kind of arrow with a rubber suction-cup end, of course. What, you think my parents would have let me play with a real bow and arrow? It was one of the things I was maddest at them about.

But I wasn't feeling a bit brave on the first day of kindergarten. For the first day, our moms walked us there and picked us up. After that, we were supposed to walk there ourselves. I disapproved of this because I was 100 percent sure I would get lost. The way to school was a straight line, but I was still sure. All my life, I've worried that even if you take the right route, you might suddenly end up in the wrong place. What if the sidewalk suddenly changes its mind and leads you around a corner you hadn't expected?

When I was about twenty-three, I was walking down Fifth Avenue in New York City with my friend Steve Crist. I was on my way to Bloomingdale's, a big department store on Third Avenue. At around Sixty-fifth Street I said to Steve, "I guess Bloomingdale's is around here," and started to turn toward Third.

Steve, who had grown up in New York, said, "Bloomingdale's is at Fifty-ninth and Third."

"Always?" I asked.

Oh, there were so many things to be afraid of in kindergarten! One day our teacher, Miss Streeter, read us "Hansel and Gretel," and I had to go hide in the coat closet the second the witch showed up. How could Miss Streeter know that one of my worst fears was that in the night, after I went to bed, my parents put on witch costumes and started leaping and swaying around a boiling cauldron? In my imagination, the cauldron was right on the floor of our living room, with flames leaping underneath it. I don't know how my parents were supposed to keep the rest of the house from catching on fire, but after all, they were *witches*. They probably knew some fire-prevention spell.

It's odd that I never mentioned this concern to my parents. But then, when you have parents who turn into witches, you don't want them to know that you *suspect* them of anything. Similarly, when my husband was little, he was too scared to ask his parents why—he suspected—they had secretly given him a tuberculosis test, and why they weren't telling him that it had turned out positive. He got this idea from seeing a red spot on his leg.

So hearing about a real witch—I mean, a witch in a story— was bad. Especially because this witch had a gingerbread house with *candy* on it. In real life, I never got enough candy. That witch would have lured me inside right away! To make matters worse, Miss Streeter called my mother and *told* her I'd been afraid during story hour. I'm sure she thought this was the responsible thing to do, but to me, it felt like tattling.

But then Miss Streeter went away in the middle of the year,

which was even scarier than having her read about witches. Substitute teachers are bad enough when you're little. When my daughter, Laura, was in first grade, she had a substitute  a lot because her regular teacher was on some kind of important committee that required many meetings. Once, the school nurse called and said, "Laura says she's not feeling well." I suspected it was because there was a substitute again, but I brought Laura home anyway. Later, I heard her playing with her dolls. She was being a mother calling the doctor about one of them.

"She's sick?" Laura made the doctor say. "Are you sure she isn't pretending?"

But to have a teacher actually *leave*, and to have to get a whole new teacher! Miss Streeter had to move because she was getting married or something. I didn't care what the reason was. All I cared about was that our new teacher, Mrs. Mills, didn't do things the right way. Substitute teachers never accept it when you tell them that your real teacher does things another way. They always say, "Well, I'm here today, and we're going to do things *my* way." At least they go back where they came from after a couple of days, though, but Mrs. Mills wasn't going anywhere. I disapproved of this new universe very much.

"What's that you're drawing?" Mrs. Mills asked me one day.

"It's a machine to take you away," I said.

Mrs. Mills looked sad. "You know, when you say things like that, it really hurts my feelings," she told me.

I couldn't believe it. I literally couldn't. I was shocked. Something *I* had said hurt a *teacher's* feelings? *I* could be mean to a

My kindergarten class. Benjy Sax is third from the left in the top row; David Thaler is second from the right, front row. I am the one with my finger in my mouth looking sideways. At the last moment, I decided I would look cuter that way than staring into the camera.

grown-up? It was the first time, I think, that I'd ever thought about a grown-up's feelings, and I felt bad. I still wished we could have Miss Streeter back—even though I don't remember anything about her now—but I didn't draw any more take-Mrs.-Mills-away machines after that.

Mrs. Wellman

My first-grade teacher was named Mrs. Wellman. On the first day of school, in her opening speech, she gave us two pieces of advice. The first was never to jump off a merry-go-round while it was still going. "Always wait until it has *completely stopped*," she said. "I once knew a little boy who jumped off a merry-go-round, and he slipped and got caught in the machinery and was ground right up."

That got our attention. The merry-go-round in the big park nearby was famous, and we'd all been on it many times. It had much more than horses: it had a pig, and a cat with a fish in her mouth, and a goat, and I think even a deer. None of us had realized that it also had the power to grind children up if they weren't careful. But Mrs. Wellman's second piece of advice was even more surprising.

"Never try to hitch a ride on the back of a horse-drawn

wagon," she told us. "I once knew a little girl who jumped onto the back of a horse-drawn wagon. The driver didn't know she was there, and when he flicked his whip, the whip went backward and took out the little girl's eye."

Before you start imagining things, let me assure you that we didn't have horse-drawn wagons when I was little. Maybe there were still a few on farms or something, but not in the streets of Rochester, New York. I'll never know why Mrs. Wellman thought she should share this particular advice with us, but if you pay attention, you'll notice that the stories people tell are very revealing.

When my son was in sixth grade, his science teacher— his *science* teacher!—said, "Now, boys and girls, you won't find this in any books, but I believe there are already clones walking among us." And I know a whole class of seventh-graders who were told by their English teacher that the correct spelling of "dilemma" is "dilemna." Although I guess that only reveals that that English teacher didn't know how to spell.

When my great-grandfather was in first grade, his teacher asked the class, "How much is seven times zero?"

"Seven," said a girl.

"That's right," the teacher told her.

My grandfather raised his hand. "If I have seven trees with no apples on them, how many apples do I have?" he asked.

The teacher was silent for a minute. Then she said, "Either answer is correct."

Oh! Oh! I have to tell you just one more! When my uncle Charlie was little, he turned in a test that was so perfect, his teacher accused him of cheating.

"How could I have cheated?" sputtered Uncle Charlie. "I turned in my test before anyone else in the class, you louse!"

Anyway, my whole first-grade class was perplexed about that poked-out eye. "But, Mrs. Wellman, what happened to the girl's eye?" Sally Vink asked.

"I told you. It was poked out."

"But where did it *go*?"

But Mrs. Wellman was moving on to the rules for leaving the classroom. If we needed a drink of water, we were to raise one finger. If we needed to go to the bathroom, two fingers. And no one could go to the bathroom before eleven in the morning, no matter how badly they had to. This rule was changed soon after, when a certain person I won't mention (but she's a writer whom you may have heard of) wet her pants and her mother marched over to the school to point out that having to go to the bathroom has nothing to do with what time it is.

When I was in first grade, we learned reading much differently from the way you learn it now. PS 47 was an old-fashioned school even for those days, and we didn't have phonics. No sounding things out! You looked at a word, the teacher told you what it was, and you were supposed to remember it. Then you read it over and over in different stories so it would get mashed into your brain.

For me, this worked out very well. I can still remember sitting in our little reading group with our copies of *Fun with Dick and Jane* in front of us. (Yes, we really had Dick and Jane books. They weren't a joke back then.) I knew all my letters, of course, but they looked so different on the page!

"Who is this?" asked Mrs. Wellman, pointing at a black-and-white cocker spaniel.

S-P-O——

"Spot!" I suddenly said. One instant, I had just been staring at some letters in a row. The next instant, I was suddenly looking at a real word.

I honestly feel as though I went to school that morning without knowing how to read and came home that afternoon reading everything. It must actually have taken a little longer than that, but in a few days I was reading well enough to see a friend across the playground at home and scream, "I can sure read better than all those second-graders!"

"Ann, shut up!" my mother said. I was shocked. "Shut up" was one of the worst things a person could say, and here was a *mother* saying it! And to me, her own dear, precious child! More calmly, Mum continued, "You shouldn't brag about reading."

Knowing me, I just switched to bragging in a less obvious way. In any case, I kept on reading everything I could see. Pretty soon, Sally was looking for a pet in a much farther-along Dick and Jane book.

"A robin likes to hop," said Sally. "Maybe I could catch a robin." . . . Even in first grade I knew how impossible that would be. At the end of the story, Sally came home to find Puff, the kitten, waiting for her. That seemed impossible, too. On the *very day* she went out to find a pet, a kitten arrived at her house? Real parents took way longer to get the message about something their children wanted.

Soon Sally and Puff were behind me too. A few weeks into the school year, the school principal called my parents.

"Ann is learning to read too fast," she said. "It's not good for her. She needs to take up a hobby."

Reading in first grade. I don't know why I was wearing party clothes.

What kind of hobby? my astonished parents wanted to know.

"How about spool knitting?" said the principal.

I'm glad my parents didn't listen to her.

Mrs. Fisher

Mrs. Fisher was my second-grade teacher. She had light red hair and was much more jolly and kind than Mrs. Wellman had been. On our first day of school, she told us how *she* had learned to read—or at least to read the letter B. *Her* teacher had poured some water from a pitcher into a bowl, and the sound the water made was supposedly *blub, blub*. "Blub" for B, you see. This seemed confusing to me. Why hadn't kids thought the water was making a sound like *glug, glug*? What if it had fallen in a steady stream and sounded like no letter in particular? But since Mrs. Fisher obviously knew how to read, I wasn't too worried.

My family had moved away from University Park by then. Now I was in a different school, one I took a bus to. Our bus driver was a mean old man named Ted. I remember Ted more clearly than anything else about second grade. Once, for instance, he pulled the bus over to the side of the road, parked it, stood up,

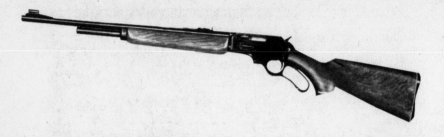

and pulled a rifle out from behind his seat. "If you all don't stop talking, I'll shoot you," he said.

I won't say we stopped talking forever, but at least we were very quiet for the rest of *that* trip.

Now, I know that driving a school bus can be a hard job. For all I know, Ted may have been holding up a toy gun. Still, I can't believe I grew up in a time where things like that were allowed to happen. If a bus driver did that now, he'd be fired so fast he wouldn't have time to turn around. At least some of the kids on the bus must have told their parents what had happened (though I don't remember mentioning it), but Ted kept right on being our driver.

Speaking of shooting: People in my generation love to remember where we were when we heard that President Kennedy had been killed. Well, I was in second grade, and I heard it on the bus going home. Ted was the one who broke the news to us.

"You've heard that President Kennedy was shot, right?" he asked when we were all sitting down.

My mother's father, David Bailey, when he was in second or third grade. The little girl is my great-aunt Jeannette. Maybe they learned to read by the "pitcher" method.

There was a chorus of yesses, but my friends and I gasped out, "No!" Mrs. Fisher must have decided not to tell us.

"Well, he's dead," Ted snapped. Then he turned on the ignition and the bus pulled out onto the road.

What a terrible way to tell children such scary news. When I get that time machine finished, I'm going back in time and having Ted fired.

Miss Bates, Miss Swang, and Mrs. Vogt

Actually, I don't remember a thing about my first day of third grade. The main thing I remember from third grade is the beautiful, beautiful bird poems I wrote that year, which I've talked about in a different part of this book. Our teacher was named Miss Bates, and, amazingly, she got engaged to a man named *Mr.* Bates. She wouldn't be leaving our class after she got married, and she would still have the same name when she came back from her honeymoon! We felt very lucky. Unfortunately, Miss Bates's wedding had to be called off at the last minute—even though the other third-grade teachers had helped us plan a surprise party for her. The rumor was that Mr. Bates had been arrested for setting fires.

Miss Bates was tiny and stern. Once, when she was yelling at us, she said, "You think I'm kidding, but I'm not. I'm dead serious." Unfortunately, that made me laugh. Only a few weeks earlier, I had teasingly asked my father, "Am I going to get any Christmas presents this year?"

"Not a one," Dad said, straight-faced.

"Are you *serious*?"

"Oh, I'm dead serious," Dad said.

Now Miss Bates said in a dreadful voice, "Ann, do you have a joke you'd like to share with the class?"

I don't remember what I answered, but at least I'm still alive.

On the first day of fourth grade, as we waited to go into the building, David Lee said to me, "You know what you are? You're a big hunk of mucus." My friends and I thought that was delightfully funny. Fourth grade was a good year for humor. Our teacher, Miss Swang, did lots of great stuff like standing on her desk and screaming when she made a mistake in class. She also had good penalties if you lost a spelling bee or other class competition. Once I had to walk all the way to the principal's office, counting my steps aloud, and then go in and tell the principal how many steps it had taken me to get there.

Mrs. Vogt, my fifth-grade teacher, wasn't a bit funny, except inadvertently. She liked to alternate between classic and nonclassic children's books when she read aloud to us. One month it would be Enid Blyton's *Five Get Into Trouble*, the next month *Caddie Woodlawn*.

"Do you see how much better *Caddie Woodlawn* is than the *Five* book?" Mrs. Vogt would ask, running her finger along a page. "Even the paper is better quality."

Mrs. Vogt could start with a chance remark to the class and rev up into full-fledged yelling in about ten seconds. Another bad thing: she didn't believe that I knew the words I knew. At some point during the year, I had to write a report on Benjamin Franklin. In one section of the report, I said that when Ben Franklin went to Paris, he was "lionized"[1] by the French. Okay, I only knew what the word meant because my father had used it—and maybe it was a show-offy word to use in a report—but I *did* know what it meant.

"What did you say?" Mrs. Vogt asked when I read the report to the class.

"Lionized," I repeated.

"That's a big word for a little girl," Mrs. Vogt said suspiciously.

Oh, she was a cranky one. Looking back, I wonder if she was depressed or in constant pain or something. Once I wore a Peanuts sweatshirt with Snoopy on the front and the quote "Sometimes you just need someone to bite" on the back. Mrs. Vogt read the back and said morosely, "I feel that way a lot of the time."

My mother always tells me, "But Mrs. Vogt really taught you math." I don't know if that's a good enough excuse—and anyway, it's not even true! I don't know *any* math! In eleventh grade, I got a 44 percent on my end-of-the-year math exam, and when I retook the exam, I got a 43 percent.

That's a little score for a big girl.

---

1. Lionize: *to treat a person like a celebrity. It* WAS *a show-offy word. I would never use it now.*

My father's father, Crosby Hodgman, when he was in fifth or sixth grade.

Mr. Collins

Sixth grade was the last year we had just one teacher; after that, we had a different teacher for each subject. On the first day of sixth grade, our teacher, Mr. Collins, held up a kind of bug that you've probably seen before—the kind that rolls into a little ball when you pick it up. "Does anyone know this bug's name?" he asked.

Answers jumped at him from all over the room.

"Potato bug."

"It's a potato bug."

"Potato bug."

I sat and waited, like a hungry spider. I knew my time would come.

"Actually, this isn't called a potato bug," said Mr. Collins. "Any other ideas?"

"It's a sow bug," I said.

Well, okay! I knew pretty much about bugs, and it *was* a sow bug! Not that big a deal, right? But maybe correcting the whole class isn't the *best* way to make new friends. And then, a little later the same day, Mr. Collins mentioned something about rabbits being rodents.

Instantly my hand darted into the air. "Rabbits aren't rodents," I told him proudly. "They're lagomorphs."

"Wow," said Mr. Collins. "I didn't know that. I guess *I* learned something today." And I sat back proudly in my seat.

Again—not that big a deal. But still. Who corrects the *teacher*, in front of the whole class, on the first day of school, and is *proud* of it?

Not me, that's for sure. I must be talking about some other girl.

sports

My elementary-school gym classes pretty much finished sports off for me. Our gym teacher was a ten-foot-tall man who never smiled and who carried a bloody ax, as I recall. I remember his name, but I'm not even going to think about it: it makes me too scared. I'll just call him the Gym Teacher.

The Gym Teacher's favorite game was called Try Until You Get It. This was a simple routine where everyone in the class kept shooting basketballs until we made a basket, except that I never made a basket. Since the class wasn't allowed to leave until all of us had made baskets, the other kids stood around hooting and jeering while I flopped and floundered under the hoop long after the lunch bell had rung.

That was how I learned that sports are what you do to humiliate yourself in front of people who are better than you. Or it was *another* of the ways I learned it. By second grade I was already pretty sure that I wasn't going to be much of an athlete. By third grade, I was beginning to suspect that being good at sports was the best way to be popular. And by fourth grade, I was sure of it.

Up until fourth grade, gym class was just games and exercise. We played things like Flowers and the Wind, the kind of game I would have thought up if I'd been a game-thinker-upper. Half the class—the Wind team—would line up across one end of the gym. The other half would think up the name of a flower and then line up in front of the Wind. The Wind would gather into a huddle and whisper urgently together, then line up again and call out the names of different flowers.

"Rose!" (They always guessed rose first.)

The flowers would stand there.

"Tulip!"

Nothing.

"Dandelion!"

Still nothing.

And so on, until someone on the Wind team said, "Forsythia!" And then the Flowers would race back toward the safe end of the gym while the Wind tried to catch them. If anyone from the Wind team tagged a member of the Flower team, that person had the Wind team.

I bet this sounds kind of lame, doesn't it? But I liked it, especially because I knew lots of flower names that the Wind kids couldn't guess—names like "hepatica" and "trillium." (My father and grandfather were serious gardeners.) I could think of flowers that were so unusual, the Wind team would get really mad at how long they had to stand there guessing.

But in fourth grade, games like Flowers and the Wind disappeared like—well—flowers in the wind. In fourth, gym turned into sports.

I don't have any gym pictures. Here, though, you can see my brave, athletic friend Lila fiercely walking on an overturned rope spool. Behind her, looking terrified, are me and my sisters, Cathy and Cornelia. Cathy and I are especially scared because we know it's our turn after Lila.

I had noticed for a long time that my body wasn't interested in doing stuff it wasn't used to. When I was in preschool, there was no local library near where we lived. Instead, a bookmobile came to our neighborhood once a week. It was like a bus, but with (duh) bookshelves and a librarian inside. Every week, my mother would bring me to the bookmobile, where I would join other preschoolers from the neighborhood. We'd all climb aboard for story hour and then check out a few books to take home.

"Now, I want you to sit on the floor Indian-style," the librarian told us on the first day. She meant sitting with your legs folded, or what preschool teachers sometimes call "crisscross, applesauce." Whatever she called it, I didn't like it. The other kids obediently folded their legs into pretzels, and I tried to do the same. But my legs wouldn't stretch the way theirs did. Sitting cross-legged felt too bumpy and strained. Halfway through my first story hour ever, I thought to myself, "I hate this. I'm never going to sit this way again." And I never did—not until I was a grown-up, anyway.

At around the same time, my father tried to teach me how to hit a softball. He would patiently throw the ball, and I would swing the bat in some vague direction and miss the ball by a mile. "Keep your eye on the ball, Ann," Dad would say, over and over. But *why*? Why were we doing this stupid activity in the first place? It wasn't related to anything I was interested in. We didn't have a TV when I was in preschool and kindergarten, so I had never seen a baseball game. But even if I had, it would have made me insane with boredom. A lot of grown-ups waiting in line to hit a *ball*? Why didn't they just hit themselves in the head while they were at it?

I'd rather be
reading. Duh!

Let me say right here that I do like sports now. I'm an ice-hockey goalie, and I feel as though I wasted the first forty years of my life not playing hockey. Let me say, too, that if I had wanted to be good at sports when I was a kid—or at least decent—I know I could have done it. Three-quarters of being good at a sport (okay, decent) comes from paying attention and practicing. The trouble was that I didn't want to pay attention, and I didn't want to practice. I wanted to read.

But you couldn't read in gym! Even if you had a doctor's note excusing you from gym, you still had to sit up against the wall and watch everyone else. There were many things to dread in gym class, and every year there were more of them. For example, there were way too many times when you had to throw yourself around or step into space. Backward somersaults in second grade—more bumps!—became cartwheels in third grade; then they added a balance beam in fourth grade, and that horrible "pommel horse" in fifth, and before you know it, I was in high school, stuck in midair on the parallel bars. I don't like being in the air. I like being on the ground, where gravity *wants* me to be.

Some of my friends actually enjoyed flipping themselves around, though. My two-houses-down-the-street friend, Robin, loved it. She also loved doing cartwheels, which I've never been able to learn and never will. (Okay, maybe if I practiced for ten years, but I won't do that.) We'd be sitting on the lawn talking, and suddenly Robin would jump up and do a bunch of backflips. I've never been happier than the time she started to cartwheel, threw her landing hand to the ground, yelped, and collapsed. "I put my hand into dog doo!" she shrieked.

 That's what should happen to everyone who suddenly does a cartwheel.

The Absolute Worst!

But the worst gym unit was softball. No, wait. Softball was terrible, out in the hot sun on a dusty softball diamond. (As my daughter once said to me, "Mom, the sun is not your friend.") But the annual Presidential Physical Fitness tests were even worse. Once a year, we had to do a lot of crunches and sprints and push-ups and stuff, and then be compared with how we had done the year before. Somehow—as we understood it—the information was sent to the president, so you were really supposed to try hard. Because you couldn't beat the Communists unless you were physically fit.

No, wait. The absolute 100 percent *worst unit of all* was Ropes.

These weren't the kind of ropes you see at summer camps—those rope courses slung between trees or huge rope nets like big square spiderwebs, where you're attached to a cable to keep you from getting hurt if you fall off. No cables in gym class! No rope bridges or rope nets. Just—well—*ropes*. Ropes that hung down like snakes from hooks in the ceiling. And that ceiling was way, way up there—so high that the tops of the ropes were lost in misty clouds. Actually, it was probably no more than thirty feet up. Still, thirty feet was pretty dreadful if you were supposed to climb that high on nothing but a rope. And with nothing under you but a gym mat.

Yet all around me I could hear the other kids twittering with excitement. Some of them looked forward to Ropes every year. How could they? Now they were rushing to be the first in line to climb.

Lines are a problem if you hate gym. If you're last in line, you have longer to dread whatever is coming. Being first gets that out of the way, but usually only kids who are good at something want to be first. Those kids are also usually the fastest. That's better for the people right behind them who can't wait to—okay, we'll just keep going with this example—climb the rope themselves. So I usually drifted toward the end of the line and felt my stomach get heavier and heavier with dread as my turn came closer. This was more than just simple Fear of Rope; it was also stage fright. By the time it was my turn, everyone else would be relaxedly gathered around, waiting for the show.

I didn't provide much of a show. I wasn't one of those kids who could shimmy to the top, touch the ceiling, and slide down in triumph. I *certainly* wasn't one of the kids who could climb to the top without using my legs. There were a couple of those kids in our class. They'd hold their legs straight out in front of them, as if they were sitting on an invisible platform, and pull merrily along with their arms. These were the same kids who could do the monkey bars one-handed. Even now, it's hard for me to imagine a person having that much upper-body strength.

I had no upper-body strength at all, so I didn't get to the

ceiling. In fact, I didn't get even one inch up the rope. I had known going in that this was going to be the case. "No sense wasting your time with me!" I could have told the Gym Teacher. "This isn't going to happen."

But I knew exactly what he would have answered: "You never know until you try."

Sometimes you *do* know, though. Even two-handed, I couldn't cross the monkey bars. I couldn't do a single chin-up. I was not going to be able to climb that rope, especially with twenty-two other kids watching me. And even if I had been able to, I would have been too scared to want to. And even if I had wanted to, I couldn't have.

I wish I'd known that it wasn't my fault.

If we had worked out regularly in gym class, maybe the kids who couldn't climb the ropes would have been able to learn. But we never did any strength training before the Ropes unit—and that makes me furious now. I came away from gym class thinking I was a weakling, instead of someone who could get stronger with the right exercises. I might never have become one of the kids who could reach the ceiling, and I definitely wouldn't have become one of the kids who could climb the rope without using my legs. But I could have done a lot better if only I'd had some conditioning.

There's no sense in getting worked up about it now. I had the chance to learn those lessons later. Besides, I don't need to buck you up about rope climbing, because I'm hoping you'll never face that kind of gym class. You may well run into a ropes course along the way, maybe on a school trip or maybe at camp. In fact, I hope you do; those courses are fun, and—as the instructors will probably keep telling you over and over—they can teach you a lot about yourself and your teammates.

But I hope there aren't many elementary school gym classes left in the United States that would expect kids to climb ropes up to the ceiling without any kind of safety harness or at least a net underneath them. What if one of the kids in my class had suddenly lost her grip and crashed to the ground from the top of the rope? Those gym mats on the floor wouldn't have been much protection.

Another Senseless Thing . . .

Picking teams.

The Gym Teacher would choose two kids to be the two team captains, and they would take turns choosing their teammates. They'd start with the best kids, of course—first the best boys, and then the best girls.

"Peter Elliot."

"Jeff Dorsett."

"Ted McInarnie."

"Peggy Siebert."

And so on and so on, endlessly, from best to worst, while we unathletic kids stood there trying to keep our faces smooth and hoping that at least we wouldn't be the *last* one picked. By the time the team choosing came to an end, we had the feeling that, rather than being chosen by the captains, we were being forced on them.

What was being taught here? Can you think of one good lesson it offered, besides the one we all already knew: that kids who were good at sports were lucky?

I can't begin to imagine why any teacher—any human being—could think this way of setting up a team is a good idea. It's embarrassing, and it's cruel, and it doesn't motivate the unathletic kids to try harder once the game starts. If anything, it makes them stop caring. Why play hard for a team captain who made it so clear she didn't want you?

A while ago, I told a fifth-grade girl the barbaric team-choosing practices of my childhood. I assumed she would be shocked at how old-fashioned they seemed. Instead, she said sadly, "Yes, I'm always picked last too." Now it was *my* turn to be shocked.

"They still do that at your school?" I asked incredulously.

"What other way would they do it?"

Well, here's one idea: gym teachers themselves should divide the kids into two well-balanced teams right at the beginning of the year. Then, for the rest of the year, the kids will play on the team they were assigned to. That will spare the unathletic kids the humiliation of repeatedly not being chosen. It will build more team loyalty over the course of the year. It may even help some kids stop thinking about how bad they are at sports and help them start focusing on the games themselves.

That's just one suggestion. A fourth-grade athlete I know tells me that it would be too boring. Maybe so! There are probably better ideas out there, and I bet lots of gym teachers use them now. But if yours doesn't, let me know. I'll send the school a letter of protest.

I mean it.

But, Ann, Wasn't There *Anything* You Liked About Gym?

Well, sure! Once a year, we had a unit of square dancing. That, I did like. Even the boys liked square dancing, I noticed. They always complained a lot at the beginning, but by the end of the unit, they were as happy as the rest of us. (By "the rest of us," I mean the girls.) Square dancing is one of those activities that don't seem as though they'll be fun. Charades is another.

I also liked swimming, although we didn't do that in gym until seventh grade. I liked play swimming, I mean. Swimming lessons themselves were scary. Even now, whenever I smell the chlorine of a swimming pool, my stomach sinks.

My sisters and brother and I, and everyone we knew, all took swimming lessons at the Perkins Swim Club. While the mothers waited in a room with some tables and coffee machines and the real estate sections of old newspapers, we kids had to walk into the locker room, change into our bathing suits, shiveringly take a shower—you always had to take a shower *before* you got into the pool, which made no sense to me and still doesn't—and then walk on goose-bumpy legs out to the huge, cavernous, echoing pool. There were mysterious marks on the floor, way under the water, and, in the deep end, a couple of regular diving boards and the high diving board we knew we'd all have to jump from if we wanted to pass into the Advanced Beginner level.

Over the years, I've often wondered about the point of the high diving board. It's fine for people who want to work on advanced diving, the kind you see on the Olympics. But why was it a requirement for us? Why did we *have* to learn to jump off it? The only answer I can come up with is that maybe they were thinking, "If these kids are ever on a sinking ocean liner, they need to be able to jump off into the lifeboats without being scared."

It took me about thirty tries to make myself jump off that high board. Time and time again, I would climb the ladder, walk slowly to the end, look way, way, way, way, way down at the water, and then slowly turn, walk back to the ladder, and climb down to the safe earth. I wish I could say that once I'd finally made myself jump, I was dying to try it again. But as far as I can remember, I never went near the high diving board after that class.

And I haven't missed it a bit.

Recreational Swimming

Once, on a very hot summer day, I walked to the swimming pool at my town's high school, which was open to the public every afternoon during vacation. I didn't have a friend to go with that day, but I was so hot and bored that I was willing to do anything—even walk more than a mile to the high school in the roasting sun. And it really was more than a mile. I know adults are always going on about how they used to walk miles to places, but a lot of times they're telling the truth. When I got to the pool, I began to regret having come at all. Going into a high school locker room alone was bad enough, but a whole swimming pool filled with kids I didn't know was unearthly bad. What was I supposed to do? Soberly swim laps, practicing my backstroke? That would have been hard, considering that everyone else in the pool was jumping around and squealing. I could hardly cannonball off the diving board and frolic around by myself . . . but wait! There were two girls I knew from my Junior Girl Scout troop— Barbie Neville and Larissa Koomen. They weren't the most fun people I knew, but they'd be way better than pretending to have a good time all alone. I jumped in, swam up to them, and said hi. "Can I swim with you guys?" I asked.

They looked at me. "We're swimming together," Larissa said after a second.

"But I don't know anyone here!"

Another pause. "Why don't you make new friends?" said Barb.

"Make new friends." Isn't that *just* the kind of thing someone from a Girl Scout troop would say? Still, there wasn't much to say in reply. Ashamedly, I bobbed away into another section of the pool. I stayed in there long enough to seem as though I was having fun, then got out and went home.

I'll give you a piece of advice I didn't learn for a long time. If you want to be included, never, *never* ask if you can play with someone. Just start playing with them. And when you grow up, never walk up to a little cluster of people at a party and say, "May

I join you?" Just go ahead and join them. It's not that people don't want to hang around with you—it's that they don't like being asked. You don't need to act as if you need permission to hang around with others of your species! Pretend you're worth it, and pretty soon you will have fooled everyone else.

Playing Outside

There were times when it could feel scary being outside, though my neighborhood was perfectly safe (except for the kidnappers I always feared were lurking around). Walking to school could be tense. The worst hazard of walking to school and back was big kids. What if you were walking along and some high school kids turned off a side street onto your sidewalk and were suddenly in front of you? Were you supposed to *pass* them? But then they would be able to hear you talking! Were you supposed to walk behind them? But then they might think you were following them on purpose! In those moments, my whole body felt stupid, even my legs.

It was also hard to walk to school if I'd had a fight with my friend Wendy. The problem there was that we *always* walked to school together. That was the arrangement. We *always* took turns picking each other up, and it would have been too complicated to change it just for a fight. Whoever was picking up the other girl would make polite, stilted conversation with that girl's mom—nothing like the regular times we were at each other's houses, when we could just be normal. Wendy was braver than I, so she was more relaxed at my house than I was at hers. She would run right to our refrigerator and yank the door open. Once she was so hungry—and our refrigerator had so little food that interested her—that she ate some plain lettuce from the crisper.

So we'd say a nice good-bye to the moms, and then as soon as we were out of sight of our houses, we'd walk to school on opposite sides of the street. I would glance over furtively at Wendy, but she was always marching strongly on, staring straight in front of her. Not only was she braver than I was, but her anger stayed more pure. Once, in a fight in fifth grade, she came up to get something out of her desk, which was next to mine at the time. (That was another horrible thing: having a fight with a friend you sat next to.) As she bent down to pull out her folder, she swiftly pinched me hard in the side. I gave a big, fake, obvious gasp of pain that was the next best thing to tattling, but unfortunately our teacher didn't notice.

Considering how much space these fights take up in my memory, it's funny that I can't remember at *all* how we got over them. Did one of us apologize, or did we just start acting normal again? I'll have to ask Wendy. We just reconnected on Facebook—after forty years.

But regular playing outside. . . . My own children grew up in a very small town with lots of woods around the houses. That provides many good playing-outside opportunities, and yet I think it may have been even more fun to grow up in a suburban neighborhood, on a regular block. The best thing about my neighborhood was the yard across the street from my house. It wasn't an actual vacant lot, but it was the next best thing. It was the side yard of Mrs. Lane and her two kids, Peter and Kimmy. Peter was a year younger than I; Kimmy was a year younger than my sister Cathy. Mrs. Lane was nice, as far as we knew. We hardly ever saw her, but once in a while she would barbecue chicken on her driveway, and the deliciousness of the smell would magically pull us over to her house.

Most of the time, though, Mrs. Lane watched television inside. That was unusual for a mother, and something about it seemed wrong. Actually, everything about the Lanes' setup seemed a little wrong. Their house was dark inside, with magazines cluttering every surface. Sometimes the only light on the first floor came from the TV in the living room. Where was Mr. Lane? We never heard anything about him, and Peter and Kimmy never mentioned him. Why didn't Mrs. Lane ever come to PTA meetings and back-to-school nights? Mothers *always* did that.

Once, dreadfully, a dog was run over in a hit-and-run on our street—this was back before leash laws. Cherry was a Pomeranian belonging to a boy named Brad, who lived on the next street. Brad found her right after she'd been killed, and the sound of his crying brought us all outside. I went across the street to ask Mrs. Lane if she had seen or heard anything. As I walked up her front path, I could hear a man's voice gabbling nervously through the screen door.

"I just ran over a dog," he said. "What should I do? I can't go back out there." Mrs. Lane said something in answer, but I couldn't hear what.

Horrified, I backed away down the front path. Now I noticed the delivery truck in Mrs. Lane's driveway. It must have been the delivery man talking to her. What was I supposed to do? I ran back across the street and told my parents.

"You have to go talk to him!" I begged. "He has to tell Brad he did it!"

But my parents wouldn't go. "It's better just to leave things alone," Dad said. "It won't make any difference to the dog."

I'm not sure my parents were right. Brad would have felt much better if he had known what had happened to Cherry, and I bet the delivery man would have felt less awful if he had faced up to what he'd done and apologized—even if it was just to a kid. But I couldn't *make* my parents go across to Mrs. Lane's house, and I was too scared to go back there myself. So Brad never learned the truth, and the mystery of the Lane family deepened. When I was a few years older, I babysat for Brad, and I always wondered if I should tell his parents what had happened to Cherry. I still don't know the answer to that.

So Why . . . ?

Ahem. You may be wondering why the Lanes' yard was the best thing about my neighborhood. And to tell you the truth, I'm not quite sure why I started this chapter with such a sad story. But let it go. The reason the Lanes' yard was so great was because it was right in the middle of the block; it was a side yard, so you could get to it without having to pass the Lanes' house; and Mrs. Lane never cared that we all wanted to play there all the time. The yard was huge, with a cherry tree and an apple tree that both bore fruit in season. (The cherry tree had lusciously glossy bark and sap that hardened into what we called "cherry amber"——hard and shiny, as long as you didn't smudge it by touching it.) Since it was a side lot, most of our parents could see us there if they stepped outside, so they didn't worry about where we were. And since Mrs. Lane never came outside, we had all the fun of playing in a vacant lot without the extra scariness.

It was in the Lanes' yard that a girl down the street, Lynn-Anne, tried to get us to believe she was four. "You are *not* four, Lynn-Anne," we kept saying. "You're *three*."

"My mother told me I could be four," Lynn-Anne insisted.

It was also here that my sister Cathy and I had an argument with our friend Robin on a subject that still makes me nuts. Robin believed that nothing was impossible. We weren't going to stand for that, and we tried to show Robin how very, very, very, very, very wrong she was.

"You can't kill a whale with a blade of grass," Cathy said.

"Yes, you can," Robin flashed back, "if you stick it into his eye."

This was maddening, although not quite as bad as the time my friend Lila had the same exact argument with *her* nothing-is-impossible friend. Lila's example was "It's impossible for people to live on the sun."

"Not if they build little ray-offs," said her friend.

Ray-offs.

Cathy also hated it whenever people talked about dog years. "There's no such thing as dog years," she said. "Dogs live for a shorter time than people, that's all."

I didn't mind dog years so much. What I hated was people saying that if a dog had been spayed or neutered, it wasn't a male or a female, "just an it."

"If you got spayed, you'd still be a girl," I would point out, unless the person I was talking to was a boy.

I also hated the time that Cathy and Robin and I were pretending to be blind. One of us would close our eyes, and the other two would lead the "blind" girl around just by talking. (We thought this training would come in handy if we ever actually became blind.) "Forward . . . forward . . . now you're coming to a curb. . . . Step down four inches. . . ."

That kind of thing. When it was my turn, Robin and Cathy led me all around the Lanes' yard and down the sidewalk; then they decided to take me across the street. "Forward . . . forward . . . ," they kept saying. Unfortunately, when they got to a streetlight they both stepped around it and kept guiding me straight ahead. I walked straight into the streetlight. I still remember how it felt when my glasses and my nose smashed into the light's concrete pole.

"What did you do that for?" I yowled.

Cathy and Robin seemed oddly unconcerned. "We didn't think about it," they said. "Sorry."

Robin and Cathy and I didn't exactly argue about our Princesses game and our Horses game, but we talked about both games so much that we hardly ever actually played them. In Princesses, the three of us were—you got it!—princesses. We were incredibly rich and amazingly beautiful, though not ready to get married; we were still girl princesses.

Half the game consisted of describing what the princesses looked like. Our hair always fell to our feet, of course, and it was always either raven-black, silvery blond, or rich chestnut with hints of red. We had petal-pink complexions and, usually, eyes of such deep blue that they were almost violet. (Sometimes they  actually *were* violet, or emerald, or some other color you never see in real eyes.) Those features, all three of us could agree on. Where we had disagreements was over our princessly mouths. Cathy and I always had little rosebud mouths when we were playing princesses, and we thought it was gross that Robin wanted "full, red lips."

But we were all in agreement about how rich the princesses

were. In fact, most of the game consisted of sitting on the Lanes' lawn and describing the princesses' possessions.

"What are their thrones like?" one of us would ask.

"They're carved out of a single ruby, with cloth of gold for the cushions. And their swimming pool is carved out of a single sapphire—no, a pearl. A single pearl." (Please note that the world's largest known pearl—the Lao Tze Pearl—weighs about fourteen pounds. That would make a swimming pool big enough for one of your feet. Also, the Lao Tze Pearl looks like a huge, white, pasty brain. But we didn't know that.)

Then we would go on to describing their princessly gowns, and then it would be time for supper.

This reminds me of when my mother and one of her best friends, Ann Hopkins, were little girls together. (I was named for Ann Hop, as we always called her.) Somehow Mum and Ann Hop got the idea that "scarlet" meant not "red" but "incredibly beautiful." They would describe colors as "scarlet blue" and "scarlet green."

Playing Horses was more active than playing Princesses, except for me. I always had to be the horses' trainer because I was the oldest. The horses were foals with long, shimmering manes and tails. Like the princesses' hair, the foals' coats were chestnut-colored, raven black, or silvery blond—palomino, I mean. But the main thing was that they were wild, never having known the touch of a human hand. This made them terribly skittish and fearful when I, their future trainer, approached them while they were cropping the tall grass in Chincoteague (really the Lanes' lawn).

I would creep up with a jump rope hidden behind my back. The foals would pace about—on two legs, of course. You can't run like the wind on all fours if you're a person. They would nervously paw the ground and sniff the wind, sensing something was wrong, until I flung the jump rope around the waist of one of them and wrestled her to the ground. She was shrieking and whinnying with fear, but not too loudly because we didn't want any of the mothers on the street to see us playing with jump ropes that way.

The parents didn't like us using jump ropes as actual ropes. "Someone will get hurt," they always said.

"No, they won't! We're careful!" Kids always know that no matter how many accidents are caused by playing with ropes and sticks, *they* will be safe.

"The rope might wind around someone's neck," a parent would say. "Can't you just pretend to lasso the horses?"

Oh, sure. *That* would really work. As if you can catch a wild mustang just by *pretending*.

Anyway, we were already pretending enough with the corral. After wrestling my new foal to the ground, I would secure her in her new corral. "Don't go any farther than here," I would inform the foal under my breath, tracing a path around the Lanes' cherry tree. Off I went to capture the other foal while the first one hurled herself against the imaginary barbed-wire fence with vigor. Sometimes she would get so tangled up in the barbed wire that I would have to come rescue her.

Training the foals was hard work too. First, I had to get them used to eating apples from my hand—real apples from the Lanes' apple tree, which was very satisfying. Then I had to get them used to the feel of a bridle (more jump ropes). Sometimes they kicked and reared or even broke out of the paddock, which required them to be lassoed around the waist again. After a long time, they were ready to learn to trot, canter, and gallop—plus a special step we called "brisking," which I had made up. "Brisk!" I would command, and Robin and Cathy would stand up straight, bend their knees up to the sky, and walk on tiptoe in a pointy, brisk way. It looked very impressive, and I think real horses should have to learn it.

Little Kids

It was best when all the kids playing in the Lanes' yard were the same age, but that hardly ever happened. Most of us had younger brothers and sisters whom we were expected to watch at least some of the time. We tried to give them roles in our games that would keep them out of the way. "*Your* special job is to guard the horses," we might tell them. "You have to patrol the borders of the corral and keep a sharp lookout. Don't ever stop patrolling! There might be coyotes outside the corral!" I have a friend whose tactic for keeping her little sister Vicki out of the way was to ask her to make glasses of ice water for everyone. "You make the *best* ice water, Vick," my friend would say.

When the little kids were playing by themselves in the Lanes' yard, they had a whole other universe of games. I once saw Nelie merrily running along shouting, "A bee stinged me! I got stinged by a bee!" She and her friends Stacy and Elizabeth also had some kind of fan club involving David Cassidy, who was the star of the show *The Partridge Family*. But I think their fan-club activities were more of an indoor thing. You can't share your love of David Cassidy with the whole outdoor world.

Sometimes it would happen that a little kid got bashed into, knocked over, or otherwise hurt. The kid would start bawling, and we'd all tense up: crying might attract a parent. The best remedy always seemed to be to let the little kid revenge herself by hurting a bigger kid. "Hit me, hit me!" we'd say quickly, gathering around the little kid so no grown-up could see her. The little kid would slap us with her soft hands, and we'd pretend to be horribly wounded. "Wow, you're *strong*!" we'd gasp.

It usually worked. Beaming with pride at having hurt a big

kid, the little brother or sister would eagerly go back to guarding the imaginary corral.

The Time We Broke the Swimming Pool

My friends Wendy Walter (in front) and Sandy Spencer. Wendy was the one I walked to school with. Sandy was the one I broke the wading pool with.

Once, a bunch of us walked down the street to Sandy Spencer's house to play in her huge wading pool. It wasn't the kind you inflate—it was much bigger than that. It had a vinyl bottom and tall sides with some kind of metal stays holding them upright.

The water was about a foot deep, and the pool could hold six to eight kids, but that day it was right in the sun. "Let's move it to the shade," I suggested.

None of us realized how heavy water is. Two cups of water weighs a pound—as my mother taught me, "A pint's a pound the world around"—and there were probably two hundred *gallons* in this pool. We all grabbed the rim and lifted. The sides of the pool ripped right off the bottom, and an ocean of water gushed out over our feet.

We took a quick step backward, eyeing one another. Then I cleared my throat. "I think I saw Jeffie Liest playing in this yard earlier today," I suggested. Jeffie was a two-and-a-half-year-old who would never have been allowed to play four houses down from his house all by himself. But he lived next door to me, and he did sometimes pester me, so he seemed like fair game. "Jeffie must have done this."

Everyone murmured agreement.

"It was Jeffie."

"He shouldn't be wandering around like that."

Then we got out of there.

My brother now says it was really my friends' fault, for not sticking up for Jeffie. "All you did was make a suggestion," he says. "They're the ones who grabbed on to it."

Yes! That's right! It's their fault! Anyway, Jeffie must be . . . let's see . . . about forty-eight. Maybe he's over it.

The Elevator

Now that I'm a parent myself, I hate to remember the time we made the elevator in Mrs. Lane's old dead elm tree. There was an elm blight going on, and everyone's elm trees were starting to die—so sad, because there had been a magnificent old elm in front of almost every house on my block. Really big trees, big enough that you could completely hide behind one of them, and now they were all going to disappear.

One of us had brought over a huge box that a new refrigerator had come in—always a great toy until it got stepped on and flattened. After we'd used the box as a clubhouse for a while, Dick Connolly suggested that we turn it into an elevator. Someone ran home to their garage and got some rope. We punched a hole in the top of the box, tied a knot at the end of the rope, and ran the other end of the rope up through the hole so the knot would hold it. Then one of the bigger boys threw the other end of the rope over the first big branch in the Lanes' elm, which was about fifteen feet above the ground. By pulling on the end of the rope, we now had a workable elevator. But of course we had to test it on a little kid to see if it would work.

"Try Lynn-Anne," someone suggested. She was Dick's little sister, the one who claimed her mom had given her permission to be four instead of three. Solemnly Lynn-Anne positioned herself on the floor of the box, and we hoisted her up high into the air. Then we slowly lowered her to the ground. The elevator worked! Now everyone wanted a turn, but we still needed one more test run.

"Cathy's skinny," said Tommy Connolly, Dick's next-in-line younger brother. (There were a lot of Connolly kids. Some of them were twins.) "Cathy, get in."

My sister scrambled into the box, and we eagerly yanked her up. At the very top of its run, the elevator suddenly burst off the rope and crashed to the ground, carrying Cathy with it. She landed with a thud, completely covered by the box.

We all rushed up and lifted the box off her. "Are you okay? Are you okay?" everyone kept asking.

"Are you okay?" What a useless question, most of the time. People always ask it when they can clearly see that you're not okay. You're bent over in pain, or frenziedly hopping up and down flapping your hands or, in Cathy's case, writhing around on the ground with the wind knocked out of you. "Here, hit me!" a couple of kids offered her, but she didn't want to hit them. She wanted to *kill* them. She turned out to be fine, just a little banged up, but I don't think you should try making your own refrigerator-box elevator. Maybe it's a good thing so many elm trees are gone after all.

Okay, that was bad, but it wasn't as bad as practically *any* of the things my husband did when he was a kid. Some of them so bad that I can't even talk about them, but I can at least tell you about the time David and his friends tried to electrocute one of their enemies. David and his friends were in the second grade then. This other boy was always mean to them, so they decided to use David's train set to electrocute him.

"We put several pieces of track on the seat of a chair in my room and attached them to the train set's control box," David says. "We were going to lure him into the house and trick him into sitting on the chair. Then we were going to turn the throttle on the train's control box to ninety miles an hour and reduce him to a pile of ash."

It didn't work. First, David and his friends were too scared of this boy to lure him anywhere, or even to talk to him. Second, their invention was a failure. "Bumpy said he could feel a tingling in his bottom when we tried it, but I couldn't feel anything," David says. So they went back to their regular non-killy games.

I wish we'd had my husband around when we were little. I bet he would have figured out some good ways to catch the horses.

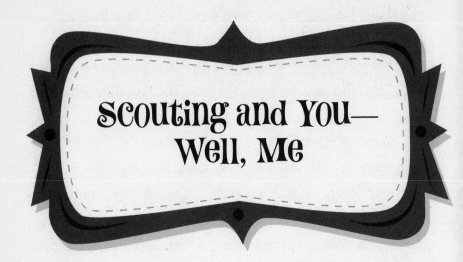

Scouting and You—
Well, Me

When I was in second grade, a beautiful song wafted over our TV every now and then. It was an ad for Girl Scouting, and it went like this:

The crow in the tree is not easy to find,
You must hunt with your heart;
You must hunt with your mind.
You must learn to be patient and learn to be wise,
For the thing that you seek is a wonderful prize. . . .
Come along now with me—a Girl Scout you'll be,
And together we'll hunt for the crow in the tree.

As soon as I heard that song for the first time, I wanted to be a Girl Scout. Imagine a group devoted to hunting for crows! It was just my kind of thing. (And still is. I've always wanted a pet crow, and I always will. Also a pet fox.) As soon as I was in third grade, I joined the Brownies, and I was surprised to find out that the real words to the song were "the Growing-Up Tree," not "the crow in the tree."

Still, I had high hopes for Scouting. Brownies had their own uniform—a brown dress with an orange necktie, a brown felt beanie, a sash, and lots of pins and patches—and their own songs and their own real-life heroine, Juliette Low, and even their own handbook. The 1963 Brownie handbook was bright orange. It cost one dollar, and it made being a Brownie sound like the most fun thing ever.

Brownies have a very special club. They call their club a troop. There may be many Brownie Girl Scout troops where you belong, or only a few. You belong to just one of them. It is like having your own home in Brownieland. . . . Maybe you have dreamed of walking in the woods carrying a pack on your back. Maybe you have dreamed of building a fire outdoors and cooking over it. Or you have always wanted to learn to sew, to make an apron for mother. But you could not do those things alone, or in a club that had friends only your age, could you? In your Brownie troop you tell your leaders the things you have always wanted to do, and they help you do them.

In fact, I had never dreamed of walking in the woods carrying a pack, or "making an apron for mother." All my sewing projects consisted of getting started on something ambitious—a sock puppet! a dress for my doll!—and then asking "mother" to finish them for me when they got too complicated. But I *had* always wanted to be in a club. And when I saw a recipe in the Brownie handbook for taffy apples—well! Making candied apples *was* something I had always wanted to do. And the camping chapter made camping sound like a lot more fun than just carrying a pack. "You may take care of a little wild animal for awhile. Or you may gather berries. You learn how to make jam from the berries."

Jam! Taffy apples! The Land of Let's Pretend! Grinding paint out of colored rocks! It *did* sound like Brownieland. I was so excited that even before my first Brownie meeting, I asked my parents if I could try out the taffy apple recipe.

To make a taffy apple, said the handbook, you took a peeled apple and stuck a pointed stick through it. The stick had to be green, of course, so it wouldn't burn easily. I approved of that; it sounded like good woods-manship. Then you rolled the apple in brown sugar and slowly toasted it over hot coals. "The sugar will melt and form a hard coat around the apple," the handbook promised. "Turn the stick around so that the sugar cooks evenly."

It sounded like magic. Just melting brown sugar would turn it into the delicious, shiny, hard, bright-red candy coating on apples you got at fairs? I coated my apple in sugar, planted myself next to the grill, and waited for the transformation.

It never came, of course. The brown sugar got damp from the apple, and some of it dripped off into the fire. Some of it *kind* of melted, but only in the way I had seen brown sugar melt when my mother made glazed carrots. It never hardened, because the apple was too wet. It certainly didn't turn into a hard, bright-red candy shell. And meanwhile, the apple was getting soft and brown itself. What I ended up with was a half-baked apple with some half-burned brown sugar on parts of it.

Through my disappointment, I realized that deep down I'd suspected that the path from brown sugar to red candy might be more complicated than just putting an apple on a stick. It made me even angrier that a book had promised something I knew might not be true and I had *still* decided to believe it.

But I didn't give up hope for Scouting. When, at our first meeting (in the cafeteria at my elementary school), we had little candy bars for our snack, I knew I had found Brownieland. We never had little candy bars at home.

But where were the wild animals and the berries? It seemed as though mostly what we did week after week was sit in the cafeteria. (My friend Patty says that in her Brownie troop, they "collected dues, drank juice, and went home.") We weren't going to be able to go outside until we had made our Sit-Upons. They were our first project and, like all Brownie projects, they were divided up into several meetings' worth of work. The first week, we brought in magazines and newspapers. The next week, we cut out squares of oilcloth—that thick, waterproof stuff that picnic tablecloths are sometimes made out of. Then all the squares had to go home with Mrs. Gershon, the troop leader, so she could punch holes in them for the following week. Brownies' tender little Brownie fingers might have gotten pierced or cut if they had tried to make the holes themselves!

The following week, we layered the oilcloth squares with magazines, sewed them together with thick, bright yarn, and wrote our names on them. Now that our Sit-Upons were ready, we could go outside and sit upon them. Of course, it was mid-November by then. The ground was awfully cold even through layers of oilcloth and magazines, and there weren't going to be a lot of wild animals and berries on the school fields.

Most Brownie projects seemed to dissolve away in the same fashion. It was easier to sit in the cafeteria and learn Brownie songs or different embroidery stitches. The only project I really remember liking was the time Mrs. Gershon went to an optician's and got lots and lots of eyeglass lenses. We lined them with cut-out magazine photos of flowers, painted the backs with gold paint, attached pins, and presto! Lens-shaped flower brooches for Mother's Day!

Then there were the Girl Scout Cookie sales. We were supposed to go door to door taking orders, but my sisters and I could never bear the thought of doing that, so Mum nicely bought all the cookies we were supposed to sell and put them in the basement freezer. It was worth eating Thin Mint cookies month after month, as long as we hadn't had to sell them to the neighbors.

Being a Brownie Adult

I don't mean to sound as though my Brownie leaders didn't do a good job. When I grew up, I helped some Brownie leaders in Laura's troop, and I found out that it's hard, hard work coming up with projects week after week.

The other two leaders—the real leaders—did the real work and came up with the projects. I mostly passed out the scissors and found people's coats when it was time to go outside. Still, every now and then, my personality would sneak through. There was one girl in the troop whom I couldn't stand. I'll call her Bettina Frost. Bettina was the kind of girl who would tattle even if she hadn't exactly witnessed the thing she was tattling about.

"I saw some kids running down the hall, and I couldn't see who it was, but they were running really fast. . . ." That kind of thing. She was also mean to anyone who wasn't her best friend, and she sassed the Brownie leaders constantly.

"You can call me Mrs. Donohue, or you can call me Mrs. Rudman," the leader of the troop told the girls on the first day. (Donohue was her last name; Rudman was her husband's last name. These things get complicated.) "It's up to you."

"Can we call you Nancy?" asked Bettina.

"Uh, no," said Mrs. Donohue after a second.

"Why not? That's your name, too."

"The choices are Mrs. Donohue or Mrs. Rudman," said Mrs. Donohue in a level voice. She had taught fifth grade, and nothing flustered her.

But Bettina wouldn't let it go. She kept needling and needling until I got so mad on Mrs. Donohue's behalf that I couldn't help myself. The minute Bettina's back was turned, I made a horrible face at her.

"That wasn't a very nice thing to do," said one of the Brownies, her voice trembling.

"Well, *she* started it," I said.

A *mom* saying that about a *second-grader*! Now I would *never* get into Brownieland! Right away I was ashamed of myself. I walked quickly down to the other end of the room and pretended to do something useful.

Bettina got her revenge later that year when we went on a Brownie camping trip. Oh, how terrible that trip was. It rained the whole time. One of the girls got her belt knotted up and couldn't get it untied in time and wet her pants. The moms on the trip had to sneak her some new pants without letting any of the other girls find out, which wasn't easy to do. I had to go through the girl's backpack while everyone else in the tent watched.

"What are you getting?" asked Bettina, who was in my tent (of course).

"Oh, Callie just needs something from here," I said vaguely.

"What is it? Why can't she get it herself?"

"She'll be back in a minute," I said. "Why don't you guys go over to the other tent and help them set up their stuff?"

"Why are you taking pants out of there?" was Bettina's answer.

Then Laura left her new flashlight at the campfire and cried and cried, even though I kept telling her it didn't matter. At bed-time, some of the girls accidentally-on-purpose rolled off their cots and out of the tent onto the ground. And naturally, some of them didn't go to sleep at all, including Bettina. She and her best friend stayed up snickering and whispering all night long while I lay fuming on my cot.

"I couldn't sleep," I heard Bettina tell another Brownie the next morning. "Mrs. Hodgman was snoring all night."

The Badness of My Looks

For my whole life, I've had the wrong hair. I've *always, always* wanted it to be long and straight, and it's *always, always* been short and curly. Yes, I could have grown it. And some-times I tried. But it always ended up looking like a cocker spaniel's ears, and I always ended up cutting it short. The last time I tried growing it, when I was about thirty-eight, my stylist said, "I hope you've learned your lesson. Never try this again."

When I was your age, I used to think that at least short, curly hair would come into style at some point. Maybe I was WASTING MY WHOLE CHILDHOOD having the wrong hair, but once I got to high school, surely it would be my turn. And then, once I was in high school, I thought that maybe it would happen in college. And then, in college, "Well, once I've graduated and gotten married and had kids, I won't care about that kind of thing anymore."

I hate to tell you this, but you never outgrow caring how you look. Even at this ancient age, I still can't believe that from now until I die, the only way I'll ever be able to have long, straight hair is if I get a wig. At some point, though, you outgrow the idea that it's worth trying to *change* how you look. So now that I'm in my fifties and there are great ways to straighten hair—really make it as straight as a sheet of glass—I probably won't bother. Trying

Nelie had the straightest hair of the three girls in my family. She could braid it and everything. Cathy once told me, "I like Nelie's hair best, then mine, then yours."

to stay blond(ish) takes enough time and money. I can't start doing even more stuff to my hair.

But boy, did I mess around with it when I was a girl.

Until fourth grade, I wasn't allowed to grow my hair. Mum thought that long hair wasn't suitable on little girls, and it's true that back then there was usually only one girl per class who had really long hair. But I hated having short hair, especially short bangs. I didn't like the look of my big white mushroom of a forehead staring out from under a little fringe of bangs. I always wanted my bangs to be growing straight into my eyes—another thing that my mother hated. "Get your hair off your face," she would say. Mothers always want you to get your hair off your face and to smile for the camera. Some mornings, my bangs looked so short that I suspected Mum had snuck into my bedroom at night and secretly cut them to avoid our having another argument.

Meanwhile, my friend Muffy was the girl in my class with beautiful waist-length straight chestnut hair that everyone wanted to play with and comb and style. Muffy was so lucky! She had had years to grow her hair, whereas by the time mine got long, I would be, like, twelve.

But fourth grade arrived at last, and I started growing my hair. And right away I realized that I was going to have problems with it. Curly hair grows out, not down. Little snips of curls would spring up on one side of my head, or a chunk of my bangs would flip into the air like a chorus line. How could I keep my hair *flat?*

The Straightening Experiments

The first thing I tried, in fifth grade, was hairnets. I bought some hairnets and some special tape at Neisner's, the local five-and-ten. After I had washed my hair, I would gunk it up with Dippity-do, comb it down flat, carefully spread a hairnet over it, and tape it down with the pink hair tape that some people used to make Dippity-do spit curls. At about the same age, my husband, David, was using the perforated plastic bags grapes came in to hold his hair down so it wouldn't stick up—

Hey, WAIT A MINUTE. You've never heard of Dippity-do? How can that be, when there were so many TV commercials for it in my childhood and you can still buy it at the Vermont Country Store? Well, Dippity-do is a primitive styling gel. It's clear green and comes in a jar. You can comb it through wet hair to give it more body, or you can comb it through wet hair and then set the hair on curlers, and they'll hold the curl better. (And don't tell me you've never heard of curlers, because I know that's a lie.) Or you can take little Dippity-do'd pinches of hair, twist them into points, and tape them to your cheeks. In theory, when your hair dries, you'll have cute little spit curls punctuating your face, like a girl from the 1920s. Who *wants* cute little spit curls? That I can't answer.

And why are they called spit curls? Because before Dippity-do came along, women would shape the curls by licking their fingers and then twisting the hair into place. It probably didn't work very well.

So anyway, for my first attempt at straight hair, I used the Dippity-do and the pink tape holding down the hairnet. When I woke up the next morning, the Dippity-do had dried into a stiff lacquer that was fun to brush out. And it left my hair in a sort of mat that satisfied me for a while.

Then I started to think that the pink tape wasn't strong enough. I could peel it off my skin easily, after all, so how hard could it be holding down my hair? I decided to switch to something tougher: masking tape. And yes, masking tape really, really stuck to my neck. Ripping it off my skin every morning was something I dreaded. Especially when the tape started taking my skin off with it because it had caused a rash all the way around my neck. Until the rash healed, I looked like someone who'd been beheaded and then had her head put back on. Even *I* didn't think straight hair was worth a crusting, oozy ring around my neck.

Ironing was next. An older girl told me about this when we

were on vacation. "You just set the iron to 'cool' and put your head on the ironing board," she said. "It works great."

And it might have, if my hair had been longer or I'd had someone to help me. But as it was, the iron was about three inches from my face when I tried ironing my bangs, and when I tried to do the back of my head—spreading my hair out with my left hand and ironing with my right—I realized that I wasn't flexible enough.

There was also supposed to be something about using giant curlers—even orange juice cans, some girls said. But my hair wasn't long enough for that yet. And none of these remedies was actually making it straight. It was just . . . flat. It must have looked awful, and I don't know how my parents kept from saying something about it.

For my own sake, I'm thankful that at exactly the same age, my friend Martha (we met as grown-ups) got a "fall" from a dime store—thankful because it shows that I wasn't the only one doing nutty stuff with my hair. A fall was a big hank of fake hair that you clipped into your own hair to make it look longer. The fall Martha got was a rich chestnut that didn't match her real hair at all. "But I wore it all the time, and I kept shaking my head so it would bounce around," she told me. And her mother never said a word either! I wonder if I could have been as tactful with my own kids.

Although maybe it wouldn't have come up. When I had kids of

my own, I decided that they could wear whatever they wanted as long as most of the other kids were wearing the same thing. I didn't want them to have to wait and wait to be able to wear whatever everyone else was already wearing. If most of the other kids had a certain kind of shoe or shirt or whatever, that meant most of the other moms thought it was okay. Why shouldn't I say it was okay, too?

So I let my daughter start growing her hair as soon as she asked to, which was when she was four. For girls that age, long hair and a good collection of Barbies are like money. The more you have, the richer you are. Laura didn't play much with her Barbies, but at least when other girls asked to see them, she had a few ready for them. And by kindergarten, at least she could have ponytails and side ponytails—a big look among kindergartners, for some reason. By first grade, she could braid her hair. I never did learn how to French-braid it, though. I wasn't *that* good a mother.

I also let Laura and John get their ears pierced when they wanted to, and then double-pierced in Laura's case. (Then she also got her belly button pierced when she was thirteen, because I guess I *am* that good a mother.) Why not? I had spent years and years wanting pierced ears when I was young. I even tried to pierce them myself a few times, with a sterilized needle and an ice cube, but I always chickened out.

In my church, the Sunday Schoolers always got little

cardboard boxes, called "mite boxes," at the beginning of Lent. We were supposed to fill them with money we had saved by not buying things like candy; then the money would go to poor children. When I was in fifth grade, I used some of my mite box money to buy "pierced look" earrings—cherry-sized fuchsia plastic balls on long gold wires that clamped painfully onto my earlobes. I had a feeling that Mum wouldn't find them as attractive as I did, so I waited to put them on until I was at school.

The Shoe Problem

The other ongoing battles I had with Mum were over my shoes. I wasn't allowed to wear loafers until fourth grade, even though every other girl in my school had been *born* wearing them. And in winter, I couldn't wear "shoe boots" until sixth grade; I had to wear dumb rubber boots that went on *over* my shoes. They were big and cloddy-looking compared with trim shoe boots, which were too tight to fit shoes under. There was a lot of snow in Rochester, so I had plenty of time to be mad about this.

The funny thing is that almost as soon as I could wear loafers, I stopped wanting them. They weren't exactly in style anymore.

A goofy picture of me in my non-shoe boots in fifth grade. They were white and were meant to disguise the fact that you were wearing shoes under them. We called them "fake shoe boots" at school.

The Best Dresses

I did have some clothes that I liked, of course. The two best dresses I've ever owned in my life were ones I had as a girl. They were better by far than my wedding dress, which—to my endless regret—I took about an hour to pick out because I wanted to get the search over with.

Both of these dresses were bought for dancing school, which we all started in sixth grade. This was ballroom dancing school, and it was a big, big deal. Like playing tennis, it was one of those things you just *had* to do, except that I hated tennis so, so much that I refused to learn it. Dancing school was directed by a haughty couple called the Vincents, who had fake-rich accents and who always stood up very straight. The classes were held on Friday afternoons in a local private school gym. All the girls wore party dresses, white tights (or pantyhose in eighth grade), and white gloves. The boys wore jackets and ties—and, I guess, pants and shoes, but I never noticed anything except their jackets and ties.

We would form two big circles—the boys' circle on the inside, the girls' on the outside. Mr. Vincent would clap his hands sharply, and the boys would move eight places to the right. The eighth girl they landed on was the one they had to dance with.

"Gentlemen, a stiff West Point bow, please," Mr. Vincent would bellow forth, and the boys would bob awkwardly in front of the girls. Then music would well up from somewhere, and we would start dancing. At the end of the afternoon, we would form a receiving line—except that it was really more of a departing line—to shake hands with Mrs. Vincent and the chaperones.

"Thank you very much, Mrs. Vincent," the girls would say, making a small curtsy while shaking hands. "I had a very nice time." We had to say that even if we'd had a *terrible* time. But I usually had pretty much fun—mostly because a lot of my friends were there and because there was very little choosing of partners. Once I got into dancing school's sequel in high school—a series of dinner dances called Cotillion—I had much less fun. In fact, I dropped out, and later it was hard for my mother to get my younger sisters into the program because of me. (If a girl abandoned Cotillion, her sisters suffered for it. They lost their reservation space in the class.) My brother had no problem; they *always* needed more boys at Cotillion.

But my dresses! Mum ordered them from a wonderful store in New York called Best & Co. Both of them were minidresses, of course, because that's what we wore then. The first was made of heavy ivory lace over an ivory silk lining. The sleeves and neckline were unlined. The dress kind of puffed out until it reached the hipline, where there was a pink satin sash. From the hip down, it was straight and tight.

The second dress was pale blue—no, really a better color than pale blue, which I've never thought was very interesting. It was a true sky blue printed with white scrolly designs. It had sheer sleeves of the same material, pleated to make a batwing shape. A batwing sleeve looks like what you'd imagine, but batwing sleeves aren't that pretty as a rule. The material bunches up too much. Since these sleeves were so sheer and so lavishly pleated, they looked almost like regular long sleeves unless I raised my arms. Then they unfolded into wide, sheer wings that fell all the way to my waist. Those sleeves meant that when I lifted my hand to put it on a boy's shoulder, it was something to look forward to instead of something to be nervous about. I might not have known the fox-trot all that well—and I might have been dancing with a boy who only came up to my shoulder—but at least I had the best sleeves of anyone on the dance floor.

There's no description of these dresses that can make them sound half as beautiful as they actually were. I wish I still had them. Would they fit me now? Let me do a quick calculation. . . . I guess they wouldn't, because somehow I seem to have become, uh, a little taller around the waist since middle

Speaking of fashion! Look at my father's mother, Donna Reames, on the left. That hat! I would have loved a fur muff like that when I was her age, though.

school. Maybe I can figure out a way to have the original dresses copied. Of course, I don't usually wear miniskirts now, either, and the dresses wouldn't exactly be in style. But if I could find a dressmaker to make those dresses, I would never wear anything else.

Things I Hated

People who pronounced Babar "Bar-bar."

His name is Bah-BAHR, and that's how I hope *you* say it.
I also hated it when people called sherbet "sherbert." There's no
second *r* in Babar or sherbet! Bah-BAHR. SHER-bet. Bah-BAHR.
SHER-bet. Get it right.

Oh, the Babar fight some friends and I had in sixth grade. We
had a free period and were walking around the halls loose, for
some reason.

"It's Bah-BAHR," I insisted. "The books came from *France*.
That's the French pronunciation."

"But you just say 'Zephyr,'" Muffy pointed out. "You don't say 'Zeh-PHEEER,' do you?"

"That's different," Debby answered. " 'Zephyr' is an English word, so it's okay to pronounce it without a French accent. But there's no English word 'Babar,' so you have to say it Frenchly."

Keep in mind that we were all eleven or twelve now. We hadn't read the books in years, except maybe aloud to our little brothers and sisters. All of us were the oldest in our families. Debby's little sister was four, so young that when her mother asked her please to check the clock in the kitchen, Evie came back and reported, "Still ticking." But it seemed important to get the Babar question resolved once and for all.

We must have been talking louder than we thought, because suddenly a classroom door opened and the eighth-grade algebra teacher's head popped out. "QUIET in the halls!" he yelled. "People are trying to *work*!"

It was a bad topic to have been arguing about where eighth-graders could hear us.

Once a year, all the teachers at my elementary school took their classes to the nurse's office to be weighed and measured. I'm not sure exactly why. Maybe it was for public-health reasons—a way of making sure everyone was growing all right when some kids' families might not have been able to afford annual check-ups. But *all* the nurse did was weigh and measure us. She didn't test our vision or our hearing; she didn't check our throats or test our reflexes. She didn't do anything that might have told her more about our health than just how tall we were and how much we weighed. So what was the point?

And what about the fact that this all happened *in front of the whole class*? One at a time, in alphabetical order, we were weighed and measured by the nurse. She would give our numbers to a teacher's aide, who would write everything down. And to make sure the whole experience was as humiliating as possible, the teacher's aide was stationed at the nurse's desk at the other end of the room, so that the nurse would have to speak nice and loudly.

I was an average height and weight, so I escaped being

embarrassed. But what about the kids who were over underweight, or much taller or shorter than the bulk of They had to sit there dreading it.

"Jay Barlowe," the nurse called out. "Fifty-eight inches tall. Seventy-seven pounds."

"Mike Wozcik. Fifty inches. Sixty-three pounds."

"Mary Duffy. Fifty-four inches. Ninety-six pounds."

A giggle swept the class as poor Mary, trying to smile, slunk back to her seat.

I hope that schools are done with this kind of thing, because it stinks.

Adults Who Made Too Much of a Distinction Between "May" and "Can"

I realize—and so do you—that there are times you should say "may" and times you should say "can." You should not say, "Can I please kick the desk of the girl in front of me?" Everyone knows you *can* do it. It's not exactly hard to kick someone's desk. You need to ask, "*May* I please kick her desk?" because what you want is permission to do it. And I hope your teacher lets you, because that girl is annoying *everyone* with her humming.

But there are times when it sounds stilted to say "may." When you're hopping up and down with your legs crossed, desperate to pee, and you breathlessly ask the teacher, "Please can I go to the girls' room?"—that's NOT the time for him to look at you archly, raise his eyebrows, and say, "Of course you 'can' go. But 'may' you? That is the question."

Just let me get to the bathroom, please.

And don't get me started on the kind of *kid* who made a big deal out of this.

People Who Hated the Word "Hate"

"Hate is a very strong word, Ann," Tina Leenhouts said to me once, when I said I hated onions. I couldn't come up with an answer fast enough, so I just looked at her. But if I'd been thinking on my feet, I would have answered, "It's just a word. It's not strong, it's not weak. If it's true that sticks and stones may break my bones but words can never hurt me, then saying 'hate' can't do any harm. Anyway, I *do* hate onions. And plus, don't use my name like that—it makes you sound like a grown-up."

When I was an actual grown-up, the mother of a preschooler proudly told me that her son didn't know the word "hate." That time, I was too polite to answer. But if I had answered, I would have said, "First of all, it's just a word, and it's a good, useful word. Even three-year-olds should get to express strong feelings when they have to. I'm not saying they should be allowed to swear, but they should be allowed to hate things. And second, of course he knows the word. He's in preschool!"

Kids Who, When You Drop Your Pencil, Say, "Hey, There's My Pencil That I Dropped!"

There was a boy in my class from third through seventh grade who always did this. His name was Pete. I kept wishing he'd be in a different class, but every year he somehow always ended up in mine. Any pencil that happened to roll into his view, he'd grab.

Another obnoxious thing Pete did: in sixth grade, our teacher asked if any of us had ever drunk water from a glass that had been sitting out on the counter for a while. Pete raised his hand eagerly.

"What did it taste like?" asked Mr. Collins.

Pete paused. "Well, it's kind of hard to describe. I guess the best answer would be that it tasted *dry*. It tasted like dry water."

I was 100 percent sure that he had never drunk this water. So it made me mad when Mr. Collins said, "That's a very good answer, Pete."

People Who Got Scared When a Bee Flew into the Classroom

When my daughter Laura was four, she said gloomily, "One bad thing about spring—bees again."

True! For kids who play outside a lot, bees and wasps are a big problem. If you're barefoot, you may step on one. If you're crawling through the grass, you may press your hand or your knee down on one. If you're mowing the lawn, a yellow jacket may somehow crawl under your clothes and sting you on the butt, as happened to me several years ago. If you're my dog Moxie, a wasp may sting you on the nose and your snout may swell up like a pineapple. And of course if you're allergic to bee or wasp stings, you're in major trouble if you get stung.

But unless you *bother* a bee or wasp (and wouldn't it bother YOU if a giant stepped on you? Well, that's how bees feel) it probably won't sting you. And don't tell me "I knew a girl who was just walking along the sidewalk when a bee came from out of nowhere and stung her." Because that's another thing I hated when I was your age: stories where someone "knew someone" who "had a friend who" had had some kind of experience that completely contradicted what I was saying.

For some reason, this reminds me that I once knew someone whose father had used poison ivy as toilet paper when he was out in the woods. And I really did know him. He was the father of my friend Diane Smith.

When a bee gets into a classroom, why do so many kids start screaming and dodging and even—if the teacher lets them— running from one side of the room to the other with big dramatic dives out of the way? Nothing's going to happen! The only way they could possibly get stung would be if they bumped into the bee during their mad dashes around the room.

People Who Said Their Drawings Were Bad

Again I must mention my daughter, Laura. When she was three, she was drawing in the car and suddenly burst into tears. "I wanted this to be an elephant," she sobbed. "But it's just a blob!"

"Honey, no! It's great!" I said. And it was, for a three-year-old's elephant. But I knew just how Laura felt. It's terrible when you have a specific image in your mind and your drawing comes nowhere near it. This still happens to me sometimes when I'm decorating a cake. The cake I'm envisioning is so smooth and pristine, and the decorations are so crisp and perfect, that there's usually a winner's blue ribbon somewhere in my imagination as well. Then I finish the cake, stand back, and see that what I've actually produced looks like a pile of sofa cushions smeared with icing.

That's legitimate disappointment. What I'm talking about is the kind of person who would proudly work on a drawing for hours—the same exact kind of drawing over and over—and then announce that it was bad.

I myself always liked to draw a certain kind of horse and a certain kind of girl. Here is the horse:

"Silver Cloud"
(mare)

As you can see, my horses always had very long manes and tails. This was the key to their beautiful, beautiful beauty, along with their dainty pointed hoofs. The girls I drew also had very long hair, and I didn't follow any motherly rules about keeping it off their faces. In fact, the girls' hair was always so long that it covered one eye. Why did I think that looked good? Here is my Standard Girl from the front

If it was possible, I drew Standard Girl with her hands behind her back. Hands are too hard to draw. If I absolutely had to show a girl's hands, I drew them pretty much in the style of my horses' hoofs.

Sometimes I branched out and drew Standard Girl from the side. I had trouble with eyes in profile until Judy Munter showed me how to do them. "You just do an A turned on its side and add lashes," she said. Excellent! I knew how to make an A. From the side, Standard Girl had eyelashes that were almost as long as my horses' manes.

Standard Girl (front view)

Standard Girl (side view)

Now that I'm an adult, I should really take a drawing course sometime. Because, as happens with too many girls, my drawing style froze when I was in fifth grade. And it never thawed after that. I simply have no idea how to draw a person in any kind of realistic way. When Laura was little, she asked me to draw a robber robbing someone.

"Oh, honey, that would be too hard for me," I said.

"You could *try*," Laura encouraged me. But I refused. I ended up just drawing a sackful of things the burglar had stolen and teaching her that the word for "things a burglar has stolen" is "swag."

My father, who's about eight in this picture, was a seriously good artist when he was a kid. (He still is.) One of his teachers wrote, "Kit's drawings show much more than promise." Dad never had to bother drawing Standard Horse.

All the girls in my class had their own version of Standard Horses and Standard Girls. And they were all very proud of their versions. Nonetheless, most of them followed the same script with their art. A girl would work assiduously on some drawing or other, then hold it up and say, "This is bad, isn't it?"

"No!" you were supposed to answer. "It's really, really good!"

"You're just being nice," the girl would say with a heavy sigh. "It's bad. I should throw it away." She might even get up from her desk and move toward the wastebasket.

"No, don't!" you were then supposed to say. "Give it to me. It's good. I really, really like it."

"No, you don't."

And so on.

Once in a while, if I was in a bad mood, I would break the rules of the game. When a friend said her drawing was bad, I would say, "It *is* kind of bad."

Then she would get all huffy. "Hey, thanks a *lot*! I'm glad you think I don't know how to *draw*!"

The funny thing is that a couple of years ago, I substitute-taught a second-grade class for a few hours. During free time, I showed some of the girls in the class how I had drawn a horse when I was a girl myself.

"That's really good!" one of the second-graders said admiringly.

"No, it's not," I answered automatically. "It's bad."

The *Superman* Episode Where the Mole Men Came Out of the Center of the Earth

Once my friend Moira invited me to her house to play. (We never said "playdate" back then. We just called it playing.) I had never been there before, and as we walked home, I pointed to one house  on the block and said, "What a horrible house!" It was modern in a way I couldn't understand, with big shapes all over it and a flat roof.

Well, you guessed it: that was Moira's house. I tried to weasel out of what I had just said by telling her, "I was just kidding."

"You were not," she said.

"I mean, I was surprised when I first saw it. But now that we're getting close, I—I like it! I just couldn't see it well enough before."

I'm sure Moira didn't believe me. Once we got inside the house, though, there was something I *definitely* liked: a candy jar, full of sour balls, right in the living room. I had never seen a house where candy just sat around like that and you could have as much of it as you wanted. I wanted quite a lot.

Anyway, this is to say that some of my friends' houses were

very different from mine. They might have candy in the living room, or a big, smooth carved alabaster chess set, or delicious Welsh rarebit from a jar for lunch, or wind chimes, or blue water in the toilets, or a TV that was out in the open instead of being hidden away in a cupboard like ours. It always surprised me when I went to the houses of friends who were allowed to watch TV during the afternoon. I could watch some TV on weekend nights, and I could watch daytime TV if we had a snow day or I was sick, but that was about it.

What a pleasure it was being sick back then, by the way. I had my meals on a tray, with a little flower in a bud vase in one corner. My mother would unplug our black-and-white TV (we didn't get a color TV until I was in college), carry it up from the living room, and set it up on a chair next to my bed. All morning there were game shows or sitcom reruns on the three main channels. After lunch came a horrible dry period when there was nothing but soap operas. Then my sisters and brother would come home from school and want to watch *Sesame Street* or *Mister Rogers' Neighborhood*. They'd be allowed to watch it in my bedroom because, after all, if they were going to get my germs, they probably already had them.

But I had friends who were allowed to watch whatever they wanted after school, and it didn't even have to be on the educational channel! My husband, David, for instance, watched all the TV that existed on earth back then. He watched *Sea Hunt* and *Perry Mason*. He watched *Superman*, and once he wrote a letter about *Superman* to the network in his city. This was the letter:

Superman
WDAF TV
Signal Hill
Kansas City, Missouri

Dear Sirs:

I have been watching Superman for about three years and I don't see how you get him to fly. I would like it if you would write me and tell me how. Thank you.

Yours truly,
David Owen

David and his friend John Ruth called *Superman* "Forty-Four," because it was on channel four at four o'clock where they lived. Like me, David was extremely shaken up by the episode called "Unknown People."

I watched that particular episode at my friend Rose Chikovsky's house. The main difference between her house and mine was that we were allowed to watch TV right in the daytime, without having to be sick in bed. Except that the show we watched, "Unknown People," was so terrifying that it practically *made* me sick.

In the middle of the night, dozens of horrible little men came creeping out of the ground and invaded a Western town that Clark Kent and Lois Lane were reporting on for their newspaper. Everything the Mole Men touched took on a sickly phosphorescent glow. Then, even worse, it turned out that the Mole Men were nice and didn't mean any harm—but it was too late. The gun-toting louts who seemed to run the town had put together a posse to hunt them down—*even though Superman told them not to.*

That was one of the scariest things for me, that Superman could forbid people to do something and they might be too evil to listen to him. How could people ignore Superman? Why had the possibility that little men lived inside the earth never occurred to me, and how was I going to live out the rest of my life knowing about them? I didn't even get to find out how the episode ended, because it was a two-part show and we only watched the first part. Then it was time for Rose's mother to take me home. For forty years, that first half lived in my memory as one of the creepiest things I'd ever seen.

Now, this is one of the times when being a grown-up proves itself to be very useful. Because when I started thinking about the Mole Men again recently, it suddenly occurred to me that I could track down that episode on DVD and rent it to see what it looks like now. So I did! David and I watched it while we were eating supper, and I think it's safe to say that neither of us will ever be scared of the Mole Men again.

We had both remembered them as dozens of tiny white creatures glowing with an unearthly, terrifying radiance. What they turned out to be was three small men dressed in bathing caps, gloves, and black footie-PJ-type costumes that zipped up the back. Shabby bear or gorilla costumes, that's what they looked like. You could clearly see the zippers, as well as the seam where the top of the costume was sewn to the waist.

The men had big fake sideburns and fake hair glued to their hands. In the movie, Lois Lane screamed in terror at their mole-like bodies, but in real life—even back in 1953, when the show aired—nothing about them would have reminded *anyone* of a mole. (Also, as David pointed out, in the scene where Lois first sees the Mole Men, she can only see their heads, not their bodies.)

There were other things as well. You could tell that it was day-time, not the middle of the night at all. A man in the show said that the earth was hollow, and no one corrected him—not even Superman. Superman himself was a great disappointment compared with the way I had remembered him. His costume was wrinkly, and mostly he just stood there glaring at people with his hands on his hips. When he sternly told an angry mob, "I'm going to take your guns away from you," he just walked through the crowd and took their guns away with his hands. Why didn't he use some of his superpowers? The next time someone my age says how inferior today's TV shows are compared with the shows we grew up with, I'm going to show them "Unknown People."

And the next time you watch a horribly scary TV show or movie and that night you lie there quaking in your bed, unable to fall asleep, promise yourself that when you're grown up you'll watch it again and see how ridiculous it really was. I think you'll feel a lot better.

A Few Things Grown-ups Say That Are (I'm Sorry) True

U h-oh.

After the whole rest of this book, I'm going to get *educational*?

But don't worry. I'm not planning to leave you with Some Important Words of Wisdom. I'm only *sort* of planning to leave you that way. After all, I already said you don't have to read these chapters in order.

In any case, adult advice isn't limited to things like "Show respect." One thing that happens as people get older: they gain a lot of experience about things that don't work. A two-year-old may think it's a good idea to work a hunk of chewing gum into her hair. A four-year-old, on the other hand, has usually learned that Gum + Hair = Bad. A first-grader may think it's fine to brag about what a great reader she is. By the time she's in third or fourth grade, she knows not to show off. (Unless she's me in third or fourth grade.)

Similarly, adults have done enough dumb things over the course of their long lives that they can't help having learned some useful information. In case no one ever tells you the following, I'm passing them along.

"Never Get a Tattoo on Your Face."

It may be a few years before you get *any* kind of tattoo, but you should always remember to leave your face out of it. Also, never get a tattoo of anyone's name on your face or anywhere else. What if you stop liking that person?

"Smile When Someone Takes Your Picture."

You probably think you look better when you don't smile. But when you've grown up, and you're going through old pictures of yourself to choose a few for, say, a book you've written, you won't *believe* how much better you would have looked if you had been smiling instead of staring.

Adults, especially mothers, often add, "And get your hair off your face" when they're taking your picture. I don't think that matters, unless your hair covers your *entire* face. In that case, push it out of the way so that at least your eyes show. Or at least one of your eyes.

Me (in sixth grade) and Ned (about three). A good example of why you should always smile in pictures.

"Practice Makes Perfect."

Well, maybe not perfect—but much closer to perfect than if you hadn't practiced. I'm not saying you have to work hard at everything, especially activities you don't care about but are forced to do: tennis lessons, say, or religious education. As I've said earlier in this book, why do adults think you have to do your best at *everything*?

My dad used to make me mow the lawn. Since he wasn't giving me a choice about it, he paid me ten dollars for each mowing. But he also had a lot of rules about the lawn, rules like "Don't push the lawnmower in a spiral pattern." Why did he get so mad when I asked, "Can't I do a worse job and you'll pay me less?" I still think it was a perfectly reasonable question.

If there's something you want to be good at, though, just keep plugging away at it. Even five minutes a day is way better than nothing.

And speaking of practicing . . .

"If You Quit Your Music Lessons, You'll Be Sorry Later."

I know you don't want to hear this any more than I wanted to hear it at your age. But the easiest time to learn to play an instrument—or learn a language—is when you're a kid. Your brain is still young and fresh instead of stiff and withered. And you have more time to practice—even if you hate practicing.

On the other hand, nothing should stop you from learning new things when you're an adult—except the fact that your parents probably won't be paying for it.

Poor sleepy Mum, helping me practice the piano before breakfast. Since three kids in the family took piano lessons, we had to stagger our practice times throughout the day.

"Stand Up Straight."

I hate to keep agreeing with the authorities, but this one is important. Start checking out people's posture, and you'll quickly realize how much better they look when they're not slouching.

"Be Nice to Everyone."

Or, as preschool teachers say, "You don't have to be everyone's friend, but you have to be friendly to everyone."

A few years ago, I was in the baking aisle of my grocery store when I saw a third-grade girl I knew. I asked what she was buying.

"It's my birthday," she said, "so I'm buying cupcake mix for cupcakes to take into school."

I wished her a happy birthday and asked what kind of cupcakes she was bringing in.

"Chocolate. Howie Feld in my class is allergic to chocolate, so all the girls always bring in chocolate stuff so he can't have any."

That hurt my heart.

I knew Howie. If there was a relay race on field day, he took the laces out of his running shoes. That way, it wouldn't be his fault if his team lost. Because who can expect anything from a teammate with no shoelaces?

As he ran along, his shoes flapping wildly, Howie would laugh an "Aren't-I-crazy?" laugh. No one else thought it was funny. In fact, his no-lace shoes only made his teammates madder at him. But for Howie, it was better to lose while clowning around than to lose while he was really trying. Either way, he was going to lose.

I wish I could say that when I was a kid, I was always nice to the Howies in my classes. Sometimes I wasn't, though. And remembering the times I was mean to anyone who didn't deserve it is much worse than remembering things that were embarrassing.

But cheer up. Here come . . .

A Few Things Grown-ups Say That *Aren't* True

It's not that I want you to think all adults are liars all the time, because mostly we try not to be. Of course we do tell *some* lies. We have to! If you forgot your lines in a school play, what kind of teacher would say, "Everyone noticed your mistake"? If you got a bad haircut, what kind of parent would say, "It's true that your hair will grow back, but it will take a long, long time"? Sometimes the truth is too mean to tell.

But there are a few lines that parents have been quoting for generations that *just aren't right*. And I think it's fair that you should know about them. Stay on the alert for the following.

"Wear a Hat. You Lose Most of Your Body Heat Through Your Head."

This wrinkly old theory is the result of a U.S. Army experiment in the 1950s where soldiers were sent outside in very cold weather without hats. Their heads got cold, and somehow the experimenters decided that this meant the soldiers were "losing" 45 percent of their body heat. Naturally, as people started spreading the story, the percentage was exaggerated. Now there are some parents who seem to think you can lose 3,000 percent of your body heat through your head. You can prove how wrong they are all by yourself.

Go outside in your winter clothes—including a hat—on a cold day. Take off your hat and walk around the block. How do you feel?

Now take off your jacket and shirt and walk around the block. How do you feel?

Your head only takes up 10 percent of your body surface. So if you don't wear a hat, you'll lose only about 10 percent of your body heat. And anyway, what are people talking about when they say a person's body "loses heat"? It doesn't mean that your temperature drops. It just means that you feel colder.

We're mammals, remember? Mammals make their own heat.

Of course I'm not saying you *can't* wear a hat. Go ahead, if you want to! But I never wear hats myself. They give me "hat hair," and I'd much rather have a cold head than hat hair.

And while we're on this topic: you also can't catch a cold from being cold.

And you can't catch a disease from a toilet seat, although the editor of this book, Kate, says I'm wrong about this. She wants me to warn you that you MIGHT catch a disease from a toilet seat. "What if you have some kind of oozing, horrible skin rash?" she says. Okay, maybe then. But otherwise, no—not unless you go around licking toilet seats.

"You Have to Learn Math Because You'll Need It When You Grow Up."

This is actually truer than it was when I was a kid. Kids nowadays need to take a lot more math to get into college. (I got into a good college with actual F's in high-school math. *F's*.) Still, no one *I* know uses math after college, except for a few facts about angles, and we all seem to get through the day okay. (I'm not talking about mathematicians or economists or accountants or carpenters or pharmacists or chemists or surveyors, obviously.)

Basic arithmetic is a good thing to know, though—adding, subtraction, fractions, percentages, division, and multiplication. My aunt Gail never learned the multiplication tables, and all through her life she made the most outlandish guesses.

"Aunt Gail, what's nine times five?" we'd ask.

Aunt Gail would look around wildly. "Thirty-seven?"

There will be all kinds of times you won't be able to get at a calculator, so you should have the basics in your head. Or on your fingers. Lots of grown-ups count on their fingers—why not?

"It's Important to Know Where Things Are on the Globe."

It's *fun* to know where things are on the globe, and it can be a nice way to show off (or to get a good grade). But it's not important. If you need to know where a place is, you can always look it up.

"When You're a Grown-Up, You Can Make Your Own Decisions."

So, so wrong. There are all kinds of decisions that adults can't make for themselves.

They can't "decide" to suddenly skip work for a week or two. They can't "decide" not to pay taxes or not to take care of their children. If this were changed to "when you're a grown-up, you can make your own decisions if you're willing to go to jail or get fired," it would be closer to the truth.

"In the Real World, You Won't Be Able to Hand Your Work in Late."

Also extremely untrue. Adults hand in late work all the time. They have much better excuses than kids do, too. For instance, they can say, "My child was sick, so I couldn't finish the report." Or "The trains weren't running because of the snowstorm, so I couldn't get to work." I had a boss who used to call the office with that excuse, even though people who used the same train line and lived farther away had made it to work just fine. What were we going to do—fire him?

This whole book is late right now. I still haven't written the captions for the illustrations. But look—you're still reading it, so it must have worked out.

Also, why do grown-ups call their world "the real world"? Being a kid and going to school are just as real.

"Sugar Makes Kids Overexcited."

"**B**ouncing off the walls" is how a lot of parents put it. "No, you can't have that candy," they say. "You'll be bouncing off the walls!"

A bunch of very serious studies have been done about this. And they've all proven that there's absolutely no difference in "overexcitement" between kids who eat a lot of sugar and kids who don't. If too much sugar does anything, it makes people sleepy.

"Always Wear Clean Underwear in Case You're in a Traffic Accident."

I would say you should always wear clean underwear in case you're in the middle of the playground during recess and a wind comes up and blows the rest of your clothes away. But if you're hit by a car, you won't care what shape your underwear is in. Neither will the ambulance drivers or hospital workers.

"If You Put a Sleeping Person's Hand in a Bowl of Water, That Person Will Pee."

Actually, you probably haven't heard this from a grown-up. But I bet you've heard it at an overnight or at camp. You may even have heard someone say they know someone who it happened to. Well, they didn't, because it doesn't happen.

"Are you sure about this?" my daughter asked me when she read it. Actually, I'm not 100 percent sure. I will say, though, that when I've been at slumber parties where people tried this, it didn't work. For one thing, most people wake up when someone picks up their hand and sticks it into water.

"Kids Have It So Easy Compared with Adults."

Being a child and being a grown-up are equally hard—or equally easy, depending on how you look at it.

You probably wouldn't like having to fill out a tax form. Your parents probably wouldn't like having to come home from soccer practice and do homework.

Grown-ups envy kids because kids get to take naps. Kids envy grown-ups because grown-ups don't *have* to take naps.

See what I mean? It all evens out.

A related statement often made by grown-ups is "Kids today have it so easy compared with when I was little." Then they tell you about walking to school in a snowstorm or sharing a bathroom with three hundred brothers and sisters. But aren't there plenty of things you have to do that your parents didn't? How do you think they would have liked doing as much homework as you have? Because kids today usually have way more homework than their parents did.

Being a person of any age is hard. If newborn babies could talk, I bet they'd tell us we have it so easy compared with them. After all, we can move toward our food. Babies just have to lie there waiting for someone to feed them. And since food is the main thing newborn babies care about, waiting to be fed must be really scary.

"A Hundred Years from Now, This Won't Matter at All."

So what? It matters *now*, and now is what's important.

On the other hand . . .

A hundred years—or, let's say, thirty years from now—some of the things that bother you right now will still bother you, but not as much. You'll also realize that no one remembers them as harshly as you do.

I don't exactly *love* remembering that when my friend Lisa Schwartz and I were in third grade, we attached ourselves to each other with dog leashes (clipped to our belt loops) and walked around the block shouting, "We! Are! A little bit CRAZY! One, two, three, four, five, six, seven, eight! We! Are! A little bit CRAZY! One, two. . . ."

I wish I hadn't thought it would look cool to wear a key chain of a troll's head with mink hair twisted around one of my shirt buttons.

And if I hadn't dropped Mrs. Gladstein's cello *BANG BOOM TWANG* onto the floor when she asked me to hold it for a second, my life might have been happier.

When I look back and remember some of the dumb things I've done, I want to run and hide in the closet, the way I did after telling my sister, "If you can't learn to pronounce words better, you'll be a high school dropout."

I also told my friends that I was secretly Supergirl and expected them to believe it.

I *also* had a favorite soft drink

called Orange Pee-Wee. Once, there was a dead fly in my bottle, and my dad called the company, and they said it was very unusual for Pee-Wee to have flies in it and we shouldn't worry.

I ALSO sometimes wore men's cologne I'd bought from a catalog, so that I would seem more like a tomboy.

I'd better stop remembering this kind of thing. Otherwise, even *I* won't believe me when I say that I came out fine. Especially when I think about the embarrassing things I *still* do.

Like the time I was spelling my name on the phone and the other person asked me, "*E*, as in Edward?" and I said, "No. *A*, as in Edward."

Or the time I forgot to put my car in park before I got out of it and then had to watch as it slowly, slowly crashed into the car parked in front of me.

Or—but wait. My point was SUPPOSED to be that you can embarrass yourself and still end up happy. Which, come to think of it, why should you even believe? "A grown-up is telling me I'll be fine. Wow. I'm *really* convinced." (That's you, speaking sarcastically.) But this grown-up is right!

Think about it. What would you rather hear—a story about the most embarrassing thing a person ever did, or that person's most impressive accomplishment? What do you remember more keenly—the time you stepped in dog doo on your way into church, or your tuba solo in the band concert? What do you think your friends would rather hear about, if they're the right kind of friends?

What would you rather have read about in this book?

Oh, well. There's probably no way to convince you now. But you just wait another thirty years or so, and you'll see that I was right.

And when you have kids of your own, you can tell them that being embarrassed is part of learning to be a person.

And they won't believe you.

✳ Also by Ann Hodgman ✳

978-0-8050-7974-6 ★ $17.99 US / $22.99 CAN

"It's the good, the bad and the messy in this book."
—*The New York Times*

"A ticket to, er, hog heaven." —*Publishers Weekly*

"This amusing (despite the inevitable tragedies) memoir
will have readers wishing they lived near Hodgman
so they could drop in and meet who's new."
—*School Library Journal*